Boys'
Pocket Book

Purnell

Contents

The World — Part 1

Superficial area	509,805,240 sq. km.
Area of land	144,485,740 sq. km.
Area of water	365,319,500 sq. km.
Estimated volume	1,065,599,171,700 cu. km.
Estimated weight	5,976 million million million tonnes
Diameter at Equator	12,756 km.
Diameter at Poles	12,715 km.
Circumference at Equator	40,075 km.
Circumference at Poles	40,008 km.
Speed of Earth revolving on axis	Over 1,609 km./h
Orbital speed round Sun	107,179 km./h

World Zones

There are five zones, calculated according to the average temperature at sea-level. The coldest zones are those nearest the Poles; the hottest are the ones near the Tropics of Capricorn and Cancer. Curiously enough, the Equator itself is not the hottest region. If you look at a globe, you will see that the deserts of the world lie approximately along the Tropics of Capricorn and Cancer. The five zones are:

Arctic	from North Pole	to 66° 30′ N.
North Temperate	from 66° 30′ N.	to 23° 38′ N.
Torrid	from 23° 38′ N.	to 23° 38′ S.
South Temperate	from 23° 38′ S.	to 66° 30′ S.
Antarctic	from 66° 30′ S.	to South Pole

Continents

The world's land area is divided into continents. There are five of these — Asia, America, Africa, Antarctica and Europe — plus an area known as Oceania, which covers Australasia (Australia and New Zealand) and the non-Asian Pacific Islands.

Continent	Area in sq. km.
Asia (including the major part of the U.S.S.R.)	44,011,870
America (including North, Central and South America)	42,043,470
Africa	30,233,070
Antarctica	about 13,727,000
Europe (including that part of the U.S.S.R. west of the Ural Mountains)	10,523,170
Oceania	8,961,400

Oceans and Seas

There are only three Oceans, although the Arctic Sea is sometimes described as a fourth Ocean. The 'Seven Seas', known to sailors of old, were the three principal Oceans divided into north and south and the Arctic Sea. Their areas are as follows:

Pacific	165,242,000 sq. km.
Atlantic	82,362,000 sq. km.
Indian	73,556,000 sq. km.
Arctic	13,986,000 sq. km.
Other Seas	25,511,500 sq. km.

Greatest Depths

Name	Location	Deepest point in m.
Mariana Trench	W. Pacific	11,033
Tonga-Kermadec Trench	S. Pacific	10,850
Philippine Trench	W. Pacific	10,539
Kuril-Kamchatka Trench	W. Pacific	10,382
Japan Trench	W. Pacific	10,375
New Hebrides Trench	S. Pacific	9,165
Solomon Trench	S. Pacific	9,140
Puerto Rico Trench	W. Atlantic	8,382
South Sandwich Trench	S. Atlantic	8,264
Diamantina Trench	Indian Ocean	8,047
Yap Trench	W. Pacific	8,010
Peru-Chile Trench	E. Pacific	7,974
Aleutian Trench	N. Pacific	7,679
Romanche Trench	N-S Atlantic	7,635
Nansei Shoto Trench	W. Pacific	7,507
Cayman Trench	Caribbean	7,491
Java Trench	Indian Ocean	7,452
Banda Trench	Banda Sea	7,360
Guatemala Trench	E. Pacific	6,489

World's Largest Islands*

Name	Location	Area in sq. km.
Greenland	Arctic	2,142,707
New Guinea	Pacific	899,895
Borneo	Pacific	795,130
Baffin Island	Arctic	598,290
Madagascar	Indian	590,520
Sumatra	Indian	422,170
Great Britain	Atlantic	229,849
Honshu	Pacific	226,625
Victoria	Arctic	212,197

*Australia (7,636,097 sq. km.) is regarded geographically as a continental land mass, not an island.

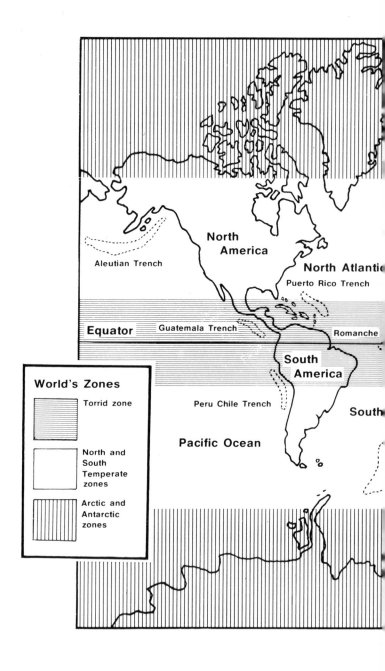

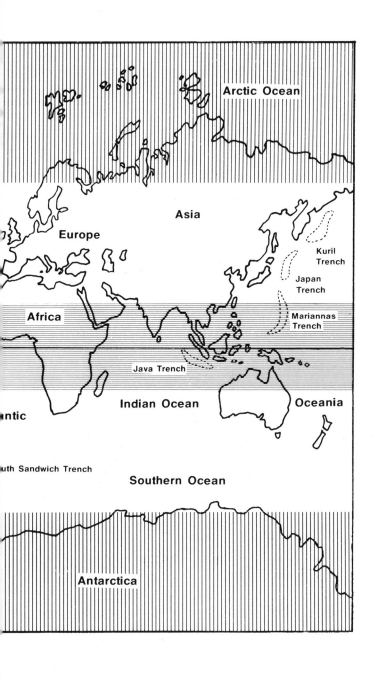

World's Highest Mountains

Name	Height in m.	Range	First climbed
Everest	8,840	Himalaya	May 29, 1953
K2	8,611	Karakoram	July 31, 1954
Kanchenjunga	8,579	Himalaya	May 25, 1955
Lhotse	8,501	Himalaya	May 18, 1956
Makalu	8,470	Himalaya	May 15, 1955
Dhaulagiri	8,167	Himalaya	May 13, 1960
Cho Oyu	8,153	Himalaya	Oct. 19, 1954
Nanga Parbat	8,126	Himalaya	July 3, 1953
Manaslu	8,125	Himalaya	May 9, 1956
Annapurna I	8,075	Himalaya	June 3, 1950
Gasherbrum I	8,068	Karakoram	July 5, 1958
Broad Peak	8,051	Karakoram	June 9, 1957
Gasherbrum II	8,034	Karakoram	July 7, 1956

World's Most Notable Volcanoes

There are believed to be 535 active volcanoes, 80 of them under the sea. The main volcanic areas are around the shores of the North Pacific and the eastern shores of the South Pacific, the mid-Atlantic range, the Africa Rift Valley and from Greece and Turkey into Central Asia, the Himalayas and Assam. Volcanoes are classified as being extinct, dormant and active. Notable active volcanoes are:

Name	Height (in m.)	Range or Location	Country	Last erupted
Anak Krakatau	155	Sunda Strait	Indonesia	1980
Aso	1,602		Japan	1980
Bezymianny	3,103	Kamchatka	U.S.S.R.	1979
Cotopaxi	5,897	Andes	Ecuador	1942
Mt. Etna	3,263	Sicily	Italy	1981
Fuego	3,835		Guatemala	1979
Fujiyama	3,798		Japan	1707
Hekla	1,500		Iceland	1981
Kilauea	1,247	Hawaii	U.S.A.	1980
Klyuchevskaya	4,750	Kamchatka	U.S.S.R.	1966
La Soufrière	1,467	St. Vincent	West Indies	1979
Mauna Loa	4,170	Hawaii	U.S.A.	1950
Mayon	2,435		Philippines	1978
Nyiragongo	3,470	Virunga	Zaire	1972
Piton de la Fournaise	2,646		Réunion	1981
Popacatépetl	5,452	Andes	Mexico	1920
Mt. St. Helena	2,950	Cascade	U.S.A.	1981
Semeru	3,676		Java	1981
Stromboli	925	Lipari Islands	Mediterranean	1974
Vesuvius	1,277	Bay of Naples	Italy	1944

World's Principal Deserts

Sahara	3,367,000 sq. km.
Australian Desert	1,554,000 sq. km.
Arabian Desert	1,295,000 sq. km.
Gobi	1,036,000 sq. km.
Kalahari Desert	518,000 sq. km.

World's Greatest Lakes

Name	Country	Area in sq. km
Caspian Sea	U.S.S.R. and Iran	371,794
Superior	Canada and U.S.A	82,414
Victoria Nyanza	Uganda, Tanzania, Kenya	69,484
Aral'skoye More	U.S.S.R.	65,527
Huron	Canada and U.S.A.	59,596
Michigan	U.S.A.	58,016
Tanganyika	Congo, Tanzania, Zambia	32,893
Great Bear	Canada	31,792
Ozero Baykal	U.S.S.R.	30,510
Nyasa	Tanzania, Malawi, Mozambique	29,604
Great Slave	Canada	28,438
Erie	Canada and U.S.A.	25,719
Winnipeg	Canada	24,512
Ontario	Canada and U.S.A.	19,477

World's Longest Rivers

Name	Outflow	Length in km.
Nile	Mediterranean	6,695
Amazon	Atlantic	6,518
Missouri-Mississippi- Red Rock	Gulf of Mexico	5,970
Ob-Irtysh	Arctic Sea	5,570
Yangtse	North Pacific	5,472
Yenisei	Arctic Sea	5,311
Zaire	Atlantic	4,828
Lena	Arctic Sea	4,506
Mekong	China Sea	4,506
Niger	Gulf of Guinea	4,184
Hwang Ho	North Pacific	4,184
Amur	North Pacific	4,023
Paranâ	Atlantic	3,943

World's Highest Waterfalls

Name	River	Location	Total drop in m.
Angel	Carrao	Venezuela	979
Tugela	Tugela	Natal, S. Africa	948

Name	River	Location	Total drop in m.
Utigard	Jöstedal Glacier	Nesdel, Norway	800
Mongefossen	Monge	Mongebekk, Norway	774
Yosemite	Yosemite Creek	California, U.S.A.	739
Østre Mardola Foss	Mardels	Eikisdel, Norway	656
Tyssestrengane	Tysso	Hardanger, Norway	646
Kukenaom	Arabopó	Venezuela	610
Sutherland	Arthur	S. Island, N. Zealand	581
Ribbon	Ribbon Fall Stream	California, U.S.A.	491
King George VI	Utshi	Guyana	488
Wollomombi	Wollomombi	Australia	481

Other falls are famous not for their height but for the volume of water which passes over them. Of these, Boyoma Falls, part of the Zaire River, have the biggest volume, some 16,990 cu. m. per second going over the Falls, yet their total drop is only 61m. 1,088 cu. m. per second goes over the Victoria Falls (height: 108 m.) in the Zambesi River. The Niagara Falls on the border of U.S.A. and Canada carry 6,009 cu. m. of water per second. Their maximum height is 51 m.

The Seven Wonders of the World
1. *The Pyramids of Egypt.* The oldest is the Pyramid of Zoser, at Saggara, built about 2,700 B.C. The Great Pyramid of Cheops was 147 m. high and measured 230 m. square at the base.
2. *The Hanging Gardens of Babylon.* These terraced gardens ranged from 23 m. to 91 m above ground level and adjoined Nebuchadnezzar's palace, 96 km. south of Baghdad.
3. *The Tomb of Mausolus* was built by the widowed Queen Artemisia at Halicarnassus in Asia Minor about 350 B.C.
4. *The Temple of Diana at Ephesus* was erected in 350 B.C. in honour of the goddess Diana. It was burned by the Goths in A.D. 262.
5. *The Colossus of Rhodes* was a bronze statue of Apollo which stood astride the harbour entrance at the seaport of Rhodes. It was erected around 280 B.C.
6. *The Statue of Jupiter Olympus.* Made of marble, inlaid with ivory and gold, by the sculptor, Phidias, about 430 B.C., the statue stood at Olympia in the plain of Ellis.
7. *The Pharos of Alexandria* was a marble watchtower and lighthouse on the island of Pharos in the harbour of Alexandria.

The World — Part 2

Countries of the World

(An asterisk denotes that the country is a member of the British Commonwealth of Nations).

Afghanistan Capital: Kabul. Area: 657,500 sq. km. Population: 17.05 m. Head of State: President. Currency: Afghani.

Albania Capital: Tirana. Area: 28,748 sq. km. Population: 2.59 m. Head of State: Chairman of the Presidium of the People's Assembly. Currency: Lek.

Algeria Capital: Algiers. Area: 2,381,745 sq. km. Population: 18.25 m. Head of State: President. Currency: Dinar.

Andorra Capital: Andorra la Vella. Area: 465 sq. km. Population: 32,700. Heads of State; Co-Princes (the Bishop of Urgel and the President of France). Currency: French franc and Spanish Peseta.

Angola Capital: Luanda. Area: 1,246,700 sq. km. Population: 7 m. Head of State: President. Currency: Kwanza.

Antigua and Barbuda: Capital: St. John's. Area: 440 sq. km. Population: 73,000. Head of State: The Queen, represented by a Governor-General. Currency: East Caribbean Dollar.

Argentina Capital: Buenos Aires. Area: 2,777,815 sq. km. Population: 27.8 m. Head of State: President. Currency: Peso.

*Australia Capital: Canberra. Area: 7,682,300 sq. km. Population: 14.42 m. Head of State: The Queen, represented by a Governor-General. Currency: Dollar.

Austria Capital: Vienna. Area: 83,853 sq. km. Population: 7.5 m. Head of State: President. Currency: Schilling.

*Bahamas, The Capital: Nassau. Area: 11,406 sq. km. Population: 234,000. Head of State: The Queen, represented by a Governor-General. Currency: Dollar.

Bahrain Capital: Manama. Area: 275,549 sq. km. Population: 350,000. Head of State: Amir. Currency: Dinar

*Bangladesh Capital: Dacca. Area: 144,020 sq. km. Population: 88.7 m. Head of State: President. Currency: Taka.

*Barbados Capital: Bridgetown. Area: 430 sq. km. Population: 258,000. Head of State: The Queen, represented by a Governor-General. Currency: Dollar.

Belgium Capital: Brussels. Area: 30,519 sq. km. Population: 9.8 m. Head of State: King. Currency: Franc.

*Belize (formerly British Honduras) Capital: Belmopan. Area: 22,963 sq. km. Population: 151,600. Head of State: The Queen, represented by a Governor-General. Currency: Dollar.

Benin (formerly Dahomey) Capital: Porto Novo. Area: 112,600 sq. km. Population: 3.47 m. Head of State: President. Currency: Franc C.F.A.

Bhutan Capital: Thimpu. Area: 46,600 sq. km. Population: 1.1 m. Head of State: King. Currency: Ngultrum, Tikchung.

Bolivia Capital: La Paz. Area: 1,098,580 sq. km. Population: 5.15 m. Head of State: President. Currency: Peso.

Botswana (formerly Bechuanaland) Capital: Gaborone. Area: 575,000 sq. km. Population: 831,000. Head of State: President. Currency: Pula.

Brazil Capital: Brasilia. Area: 8,511,965 sq. km. Population: 123 m. Head of State: President. Currency: Cruzeiro.

Bulgaria Capital: Sofia. Area: 110,911 sq. km. Population: 8.88 m. Head of State: Chairman of the Council of State. Currency: Lev.

Burma Capital: Rangoon. Area: 678,030 sq. km. Population: 33 m. Head of State: President. Currency: Kyat.

Burundi Capital: Bujumbura. Area: 27,834 sq. km. Population: 4.28 m. Head of State: President. Currency: Franc.

Cambodia—see *Kampuchea*

Cameroon Capital: Yaoundé. Area: 474,000 sq. km. Population: 8.28 m. Head of State: President. Currency: Franc C.F.A.

Canada Capital: Ottawa. Area: 9,976,185 sq. km. Population: 23.9 m. Head of State: The Queen, represented by a Governor-General. Currency: Dollar.

Cape Verde Capital: Praia. Area: 4,033 sq. km. Population: 360,000. Head of State: President. Currency: Escudo.

Central African Republic Capital: Bangui. Area: 625,000 sq. km. Population: 2.09 m. Head of State: President. Currency: Franc C.F.A.

Chad Capital: N'djamena. Area: 1,284,000 sq. km. Population: 4.41 m. Head of State: President. Currency: Franc C.F.A.

Chile Capital: Santiago. Area: 738,494 sq. km. Population: 11.1 m. Head of State: President. Currency: Peso.

China, People's Republic of Capital: Peking (Beijing). Area: 9,597,000 sq. km. Population: 971 m. Head of State: Chairman of the Central Committee. Currency: Yuan.

China, Republic of—see *Taiwan*

Colombia Capital: Bogatá. Area: 1,138,914 sq. km. Population: 26.4 m. Head of State: President. Currency: Peso.

Comoros Capital: Moroni. Area: 2,170 sq. km. Population: 297,800. Head of State: President. Currency: Franc C.F.A.

Congo Capital: Brazzaville. Area: 342,000 sq. km. Population: 1.43 m. Head of State: President. Currency: Franc C.F.A.

Costa Rica Capital: San José. Area: 50,900 sq. km. Population: 2.19 m. Head of State: President. Currency: Colone.

Cuba Capital: Havana. Area: 114,494 sq. km. Population: 9.73 m. Head of State: President. Currency: Peso.

Cyprus Capital: Nicosia. Area: 9,251 sq. km. Population: 624,000. Head of State: President. Currency: Pound.

Czechoslovakia Capital: Prague. Area: 127,877 sq. km. Population: 15.18 m. Head of State: President. Currency: Koruna.

Denmark Capital: Copenhagen. Area: 43,074 sq. km. Population: 5.12 m. Head of State: Queen. Currency: Krone.

Djibouti Capital: Djibouti. Area: 23,000 sq. km. Population: 300,000. Head of State: President. Currency: Franc.

Dominica Capital: Roseau. Area: 751 sq. km. Population: 83,000. Head of State: President. Currency: East Caribbean Dollar.

Dominican Republic Capital: San Domingo. Area: 48,442 sq. km. Population: 5.66 m. Head of State: President. Currency: Peso.

Ecuador Capital: Quito. Area: 455,454 sq. km. Population: 7.81 m. Head of State: President. Currency: Sucre.

Egypt Capital: Cario. Area: 386,198 sq. km. Population: 40.98 m. Head of State: President. Currency: Pound.

Eire — see *Irish Republic*

Equatorial Guinea Capital: Malabo. Area: 28,051 sq. km. Population: 325,000. Head of State: President. Currency: Ekpwele.

Ethiopia Capital: Addis Ababa. Area: 1,000,000 sq. km. Population: 30.4 m. Head of State: Chairman of the Provisional Military Administrative Council. Currency: Birr.

*Fiji Capital: Suva. Area: 18,272 sq. km. Population: 619,000. Head of State: The Queen, represented by a Governor-General. Currency: Dollar.

Finland Capital: Helsinki. Area: 305,475 sq. km. Population: 4.79 m. Head of State: President. Currency: Mark.

France Capital: Paris. Area: 543,998 sq. km. Population: 53.59 m. Head of State: President. Currency: Franc.

Gabon Capital: Libreville. Area: 267,667 sq. km. Population: 1.3 m. Head of State: President. Currency: Franc C.F.A.

*Gambia, The Capital: Banjul. Area: 10,368 sq. km. Population: 592,000. Head of State: President. Currency: Dalasi.

Germany (East) Capital: Berlin (East). Area: 108,179 sq. km. Population: 16.7 m. Head of State: Chairman of the Council of State. Currency: GDR Mark.

Germany (West) Capital: Bonn. Area: 248,624 sq. km. Population: 61.4 m. Head of State: President. Currency: Deutsch Mark.

*Ghana Capital: Accra. Area: 238,305 sq. km. Population: 11.7 m. Head of State: President. Currency: Cedi.

Greece Capital: Athens. Area: 131,986 sq. km. Population: 9.5 m. Head of State: President. Currency: Drachma.

*Grenada Capital: St. George's. Area: 344 sq. km. Population: 110,500. Head of State: The Queen, represented by a Governor-General. Currency: East Caribbean Dollar.

Guatemala Capital: Guatemala City. Area: 108,889 sq. km. Population: 7.05 m. Head of State: President. Currency: Quetzal.

Guinea Capital: Conakry. Area: 245,857 sq. km. Population: 5.13 m. Head of State: President. Currency: Syli.

Guinea-Bissau Capital: Bissau. Area: 36,125 sq. km. Population: 777,200. Head of State: President. Currency: Peso.

*Guyana Capital: Georgetown. Area: 210,000 sq. km. Population: 824,000. Head of State: President. Currency: Dollar.

Haiti Capital: Port-au-Prince. Area: 27,750 sq. km. Population: 5.53 m. Head of State: President. Currency: Gourde.

Honduras Capital: Tegucigalpa. Area: 112,088 sq. km. Population: 3.69 m. Head of State: President of Military Junta. Currency: Lempira.

Hungary Capital: Budapest. Area: 93,012 sq. km. Population: 10.71 m. Head of State: President. Currency: Forint.

Iceland Capital: Reykjavik. Area: 103,000 sq. km. Population: 226,750.

Head of State: President. Currency: Krona.

India Capital: New Delhi. Area: 3,159,530 sq. km. Population: 683 m. Head of State: President. Currency: Rupee.

Indonesia Capital: Djakarta. Area: 1,903,650 sq. km. Population: 148.5 m. Head of State: President. Currency: Rupiah.

Iran Capital: Teheran. Area: 1,648,000 sq. km. Population: 34 m. Head of State: President. Currency: Rial.

Iraq Capital: Baghdad. Area: 438,466 sq. km. Population: 12.2 m. Head of State: President. Currency: Dinar.

Irish Republic (Eire) Capital: Dublin. Area: 68,894 sq. km. Population: 3.37 m. Head of State: President. Currency: Pound.

Israel Capital: Jerusalem. Area: 20,702 sq. km. Population: 3.83 m. Head of State: President. Currency: Shekel.

Italy Capital: Rome. Area: 301,245 sq. km. Population: 57 m. Head of State: President. Currency: Lire.

Ivory Coast Capital: Abidjan. Area: 322,463 sq. km. Population: 7.92 m. Head of State: President. Currency: Franc C.F.A.

Jamaica Capital: Kingston. Area: 10,991 sq. km. Population: 2.16 m. Head of State: The Queen, represented by a Governor-General. Currency: Dollar.

Japan Capital: Tokyo. Area: 370,370 sq. km. Population: 116.1 m. Head of State: Emperor. Currency: Yen.

Jibuti—see *Djibouti*

Jordan Capital: Amman. Area: 101,140 sq. km. Population: 2.95 m. Head of State: King. Currency: Dinar.

Kampuchea (Cambodia) Capital: Phnom Penh. Area: 181,000 sq. km. Population: 7.7 m. Head of State: President. Currency: Riel.

Kenya Capital: Nairobi. Area: 582,600 sq. km. Population: 15.32 m. Head of State: President. Currency: Shilling.

Kiribati (formerly Gilbert Islands) Capital: Tarawa. Area: 813 sq. km. Population: 58,518. Head of State: President. Currency: Australian Dollar.

Korea (North) Capital: Pyongyang. Area: 122,370 sq. km. Population: 16 m. Head of State: President. Currency: Won.

Korea (South) Capital: Seoul. Area: 98,447 sq. km. Population: 37.02 m. Head of State: President. Currency: Won.

Kuwait Capital: Kuwait. Area: 24,280 sq. km. Population: 1.27 m. Head of State: Amir. Currency: Dinar.

Laos Capital: Vientiane. Area: 235,700 sq. km. Population: 3.5 m. Head of State: President. Currency: Kip.

Lebanon Capital: Beirut. Area: 10,400 sq. km. Population: 2.7 m. Head of State: President. Currency: Pound.

Lesotho (formerly Basutoland) Capital: Maseru. Area: 30,340 sq. km. Population: 1.28 m. Head of State: King. Currency: Loti.

Liberia Capital: Monrovia. Area: 112,600 sq. km. Population: 1.8 m. Head of State: President. Currency: Dollar.

Libya Capital: Tripoli. Area: 1,759,540 sq. km. Population: 2.94 m. Head of State: Military ruler (Col. Qadhafi). Currency: Dinar.

Liechtenstein Capital: Vaduz. Area: 160 sq. km. Population: 26,000. Head of State: Prince. Currency: Swiss Franc.

Luxembourg Capital: Luxembourg. Area: 2,568 sq. km. Population: 363,700. Head of State: Grand Duke. Currency: Franc.

Madagascar Capital: Antanarivo. Area: 594,180 sq. km. Population: 8.8 m. Head of State: President. Currency: Franc.

*Malawi Capital: Lilongwe. Area: 17,614 sq. km. Population: 5.8 m. Head of State: President. Currency: Kwacha.

*Malaysia Capital: Kuala Lumpur. Area: 334,110 sq. km. Population: 13.3 m. Head of State: Supreme Head of State. Currency: Ringgit.

Maldives Capital: Malé. Area: 298 sq. km. Population: 143,000. Head of State: President. Currency: Rupee.

Mali Capital: Bamako. Area: 1,204,021 sq. km. Population: 6.47 m. Head of State: President. Currency: Franc.

*Malta Capital: Valletta. Area: 246 sq. km. Population: 317,000. Head of State: President. Currency: Pound.

Mauritania Capital: Nouakchott. Area: 1,030,700 sq. km. Population: 1.54 m. Head of State: President. Currency: Ouguiya.

*Mauritius Capital: Port Louis. Area: 1,865 sq. km. Population: 924,250. Head of State: The Queen, represented by a Governor-General. Currency: Rupee.

Mexico Capital: Mexico City. Area: 1,967,183 sq. km. Population: 69.4 m. Head of State: President. Currency: Peso.

Monaco Capital: Monaco. Area: 189 hectares. Population: 25,000. Head of State: Prince. Currency: French Franc.

Mongolia Capital: Ulan Bator. Area: 659,970 sq. km. Population: 1.64 m. Head of State: Chairman of Presidium. Currency: Tugrik.

Morocco Capital: Rabat. Area: 659,970 sq. km. Population: 19.5 m. Head of State: King. Currency: Dirham.

Mozambique Capital: Maputo. Area: 303,070 sq. km. Population: 11.75 m. Head of State: President. Currency: Escudo.

Nauru Chief settlement: Makwa. Area: 2,130 hectares. Population 7,254. Head of State: President. Currency: Australian Dollar. (Nauru has a special relationship to the British Commonwealth.)

Nepal Capital: Kathmandu. Area: 141,400 sq. km. Population: 13.42 m. Head of State: King. Currency: Rupee.

Netherlands Capital: Amsterdam; seat of government, The Hague. Area: 33,811 sq. km. Population: 14.09 m. Head of State: Queen. Currency: Gulden (Guilder, Florin).

New Zealand Capital: Wellington. Area: 268,704 sq. km. Population: 3.1 m. Head of State: The Queen, represented by a Governor-General. Currency: Dollar.

Nicaragua Capital: Managua. Area: 148,000 sq. km. Population: 2.5 m. Head of State: President. Currency: Cordoba.

Niger Capital: Niamey. Area: 1,187,000 sq. km. Population: 5.3 m. Head of State: President. Currency: Franc C.F.A.

*Nigeria Capital: Lagos. Area: 923,773 sq. km. Population: 81 m. Head of State: President. Currency: Naira.

Norway Capital: Oslo. Area: 323,886 sq. km. Population: 4.07 m. Head of State: King. Currency: Krone.

Oman Capital: Muscat. Area: 212,380 sq. km. Population: 820,000. Head of State: Sultan. Currency: Rial Omani.

Pakistan Capital: Islamabad. Area: 796,095 sq. km. Population: 80.2 m. Head of State: President. Currency: Rupee.

Panama Capital: Panama City. Area: 75,650 sq. km. Population: 1.89 m. Head of State: President. Currency: Balboa.

*Papua New Guinea Capital: Port Moresby. Area: 462,840 sq. km. Population: 3.08 m. Head of State: The Queen, represented by a Governor-General. Currency: Kina.

Paraguay Capital: Asunción. Area: 159,827 sq. km. Population: 3 m. Head of State: President. Currency: Guarani.

Peru Capital: Lima. Area: 1,285,215 sq. km. Population: 17.3 m. Head of State: President. Currency: Sol.

Philippines Capital: Manila. Area: 297,850 sq. km. Population: 47.91 m. Head of State: President. Currency: Peso.

Poland Capital: Warsaw. Area: 312,677 sq. km. Population: 35.38 m. Head of State: Chairman of the Council of State. Currency: Zloty.

Portugal Capital: Lisbon. Area: 91,945 sq. km. Population: 9.86 m. Head of State: President. Currency: Escudo.

Qatar Capital: Doha. Area: 11,000 sq. km. Population: 200,000. Head of State: Amir. Currency: Riyal.

Romania Capital: Bucharest. Area: 237,500 sq. km. Population: 22.05 m. Head of State: President. Currency: Leu.

Russia — see Union of Soviet Socialist Republics (U.S.S.R.)

Rwanda Capital: Kigali. Area: 26,330 sq. km. Population: 4.65 m. Head of State: President. Currency: Franc.

*St. Lucia Capital: Castries. Area: 616 sq. km. Population: 113,000. Head of State: The Queen, represented by a Governor-General. Currency: East Caribbean Dollar.

*St. Vincent and The Grenadines Capital: Kingstown. Area: 389 sq. km. Population: 117,650. Head of State: The Queen, represented by a Governor-General. Currency: East Caribbean Dollar.

Salvador, El Capital: San Salvador. Area: 21,393 sq. km. Population: 4.36 m. Head of State: President. Currency: Colone.

San Marino Capital: San Marino. Area: 615 sq. km. Population: 19,168. Head of State: two Regents ('Capitani Reggenti'). Currency: Italian Lira.

São Tomé and Principe Capital: São Tomé. Area: 964 sq. km. Population: 82,750. Head of State: President. Currency: Dobra.

Saudi Arabia Capital: Riyadh. Area: 2,400,000 sq. km. Population: 9.52 m. Head of State: King. Currency: Rial.

Senegal Capital: Dakar. Area: 197,772 sq. km. Population: 5.66 m. Head of State: President. Currency: Franc C.F.A.

*Seychelles Capital: Victoria. Area: 404 sq. km. Population: 62,000. Head of State: President. Currency: Rupee.

*Sierra Leone Capital: Freetown. Area: 73,326 sq. km. Population: 3.47 m. Head of State: President. Currency: Leone.

*Singapore Capital: Singapore. Area: 73,326 sq. km. Population: 2.39 m. Head of State: President. Currency: Dollar.

*Solomon Islands Capital: Honiara. Area: 29,785 sq. km. Population: 215,000. Head of State: The Queen, represented by a Governor-General.

Currency: Dollar.

Somalia Capital: Mogadishu. Area: 630,000 sq. km. Population: 3.64 m. Head of State: President. Currency: Shilling.

South Africa Capital: Pretoria (Administrative); Cape Town (Legislative); Bloemfontein (Judicial). Area: 1,177,854 sq. km. Population: 24 m. Head of State: President. Currency: Rand.

Spain Capital: Madrid. Area: 492,592 sq. km. Population: 37.7 m. Head of State: King. Currency: Peseta.

*Sri Lanka (formerly Ceylon) Capital: Colombo. Area: 25,332 sq. km. Population: 14.47 m. Head of State: President. Currency: Rupee.

Sudan Capital: Khartoum. Area: 2,500,000 sq. km. Population: 18.4 m. Head of State: President. Currency: Pound.

Surinam Capital: Paramaribo. Area: 163,265 sq. km. Population: 375,000. Head of State: President. Currency: Florin.

*Swaziland Capital: Mbabane. Area: 17,400 sq. km. Population: 563,750. Head of State: King. Currency: Emalangeni.

Sweden Capital: Stockholm. Area: 411,479 sq. km. Population: 8.3 m. Head of State: King. Currency: Krona.

Switzerland Capital: Bern. Area: 41,288 sq. km. Population: 6.3 m. Head of State: President. Currency: Franc.

Syria Capital: Damascus. Area: 185,680 sq. km. Population: 8.33 m. Head of State: President. Currency: Pound.

Taiwan (formerly Formosa) Capital: Taipei. Area: 35,981 sq. km. Population: 17.48 m. Head of State: President. Currency: Dollar.

*Tanzania Capital: Dodoma. Area: 939,706 sq. km. Population: 17.6 m. Head of State: President. Currency: Shilling.

Thailand (formerly Siam) Capital: Bangkok. Area: 514,000 sq. km. Population: 45 m. Head of State: King. Currency: Baht.

Togo Capital: Lomé. Area: 56,000 sq. km. Population: 2.47 m. Head of State: President. Currency: Franc C.F.A.

*Tonga Capital: Nuku'alofa. Area: 700 sq. km. Population: 90,130. Head of State: King. Currency: Pa'anga.

*Trinidad and Tobago Capital: Port-of-Spain. Area: 4,828 sq. km. Population: 1.16 m. Head of State: President. Currency: Dollar.

Tunisia Capital: Tunis. Area: 164,150 sq. km. Population: 6.03 m. Head of State: President. Currency: Dinar.

Turkey Capital: Ankara. Area: 779,452 sq. km. Population: 45 m. Head of State: President. Currency: Lira.

*Tuvalu (formerly Ellice Islands) Capital: Funafuti. Area: 30 sq. km. Population: 7,350. Head of State: The Queen, represented by a Governor-General. Currency: Australian Dollar.

*Uganda Capital: Kampala. Area: 236,860 sq. km. Population: 12.4 m. Head of State: President. Currency: Shilling.

Union of Soviet Socialist Republics (U.S.S.R.) Capital: Moscow. Area: 8,650,000 sq. km. Population: 264.5 m. Head of State: Chairman of the Presidium of the Supreme Soviet of the U.S.S.R. Currency: Rouble.

United Arab Emirates Consist of: Abu Dhabi, Ajman; Dubai; Al Fujayrah, Ra's al Khaymah, Sharjah, and Umm-al-Quaywayn. Area: 92,100 sq. km. Population: 1.04 m. Head of State: President. Currency: Dirham.

United Kingdom (U.K.) Capital: London. Area: 244,022 sq. km. Population: 55.93 m. Head of State: Queen. Currency: Pound.

United States of America (U.S.A.) Capital: Washington. Area: 9,363,169 sq. km. Population: 226.5 m. Head of State: President. Currency: Dollar.

Upper Volta Capital: Ouagadougou. Area: 274,200 sq. km. Population: 6.6 m. Head of State: President. Currency: Franc C.F.A.

Uruguay Capital: Montevideo. Area: 186,926 sq. km. Population: 2.9 m. Head of State: President. Currency: New Peso.

Vanuaatu (formerly New Hebrides Condominium) Capital: Vila. Area: 14,763 sq. km. Population: 112,600. Head of State: President. Currency: Australian Dollar and N.H. Franc.

Vatican City State Capital: Vatican City. Area: 44 hectares. Population: 1,000. Head of State: The Pope. Currency: Lira.

Venezuela Capital: Caracas. Area: 912,050 sq. km. Population: 14.54 m. Head of State: President. Currency: Bolivar.

Vietnam Capital: Hanoi. Area: 329,566 sq. km. Population: 54 m. Head of State: President. Currency: Dong.

*Western Samoa Capital: Apia. Area: 2,842 sq. km. Population: 157,000. Head of State: 'Ao o le Malo' . Currency: Tala.

Yemen Arab Republic Capital: San'a. Area: 195,000 sq. km. Population: 6.5 m. Head of State: President. Currency: Riyal.

The People's Democratic Republic of Yemen (South Yemen) Capital: Aden. Area: 160,300 sq. km. Population: 2 m. Head of State: Chairman of the Presidential Council. Currency: Dinar.

Zaïre Capital: Kinshasa. Area: 2,345,409 sq. km. Population: 29.27 m. Head of State: President. Currency: Zaïre.

*Zambia Capital: Lusaka. Area: 752,620 sq. km. Population: 5.6 m. Head of State: President. Currency: Kwacha.

*Zimbabwe (formerly Rhodesia) Capital: Salisbury. Area: 390,622 sq. km. Population: 7.4 m. Head of State: President. Currency: Dollar.

The United Nations

The United Nations is the most important international organisation in existence. One of its principal aims is to maintain international peace and security, although other important facets of its work, carried out through organisations affiliated to the UN, include agricultural improvement, world health and education, economic development and finance.

The foundations of the organisation were laid at the Four-Nation Conference of Foreign Ministers, held at Moscow in 1943. The proposals were signed by the Foreign Ministers of Great Britain, U.S.A., U.S.S.R. and China. The structure of the UN was built at meetings held at Dumbarton Oaks, Washington, D.C., U.S.A., between August and October, 1944, discussed and criticised at San Francisco from April to June, 1945, by delegates from 50 nations, who put their signatures to the Charter, and came officially into existence on October 24, 1945. The UN's permanent headquarters are at Manhattan, New York.

Today, the UN has 156 member states. The independent countries listed on pages 13-20 are all members of the UN with the exception of the following which have not so far been admitted: Andorra; North Korea; South Korea; Liechtenstein; Monaco; Nauru; San Marino; Switzerland; Taiwan; Vatican State.

Two republics of the U.S.S.R. have separate membership: Byelorussia and the Ukraine.

Principal Organs of the United Nations

1. *The General Assembly.* This consists of all the member nations, each of whom has up to five representatives but only one vote. There are seven main committees, on all of which every member has a right to be represented. They are: Political and Security; Economic and Financial; Social, Humanitarian and Culture; Trusteeship; Administrative and Budgetary; Legal; and Special Political.

2. *The Security Council.* There are 15 members of this Council, each with one representative and one vote. Five are permanent members—China, France, U.K., U.S.A. and U.S.S.R. The remaining ten are elected for a two-year term. Except on procedural matters, an affirmative majority vote of nine members must include the five permanent members. It is this clause that makes the veto possible.

3. *The Economic and Social Council.* This is responsible under the General Assembly for carrying out the functions of the UN regarding social, cultural, educational and health matters.

4. *Trusteeship Council.* This was set up to administer certain territories which have been placed under UN supervision through individual Trusteeship Agreements.

5. *International Court of Justice.* The Court, which is the main judicial organ of the UN, is composed of 15 judges of different nations and meets at The Hague, Netherlands.

6. *The Secretariat.* This is the administrative section of the UN. Its principal officer is the Secretary-General, who is appointed by the General Assembly for a five-year term. Since 1946, there have been four Secretary-Generals. They are: Trygve Halvdan Lie (Norwegian): 1946 to 1952. Dag Hjalmar Agne Carl Hammarskjöld (Swedish): 1953 to 1961. U Thant (Burmese): 1961 to 1962 (acting), 1962 to 1971 (permanent). Kurt Waldheim (Austrian): 1971 to present day.

World's Largest Cities

Name	Country	Population
Tokyo	Japan	11,689,000
Shanghai	China	10,000,000
Mexico City	Mexico	8,942,000
Buenos Aires	Argentina	8,775,000
Peking	China	8,490,000
Cairo	Egypt	8,143,000
Seoul	Korea	8,114,000
Moscow	U.S.S.R.	8,011,000
New York	U.S.A.	7,149,000
Tientsin	China	7,000,000
London	England	6,970,000
Chungking	China	6,000,000
Jakarta	Indonesia	6,000,000
Bombay	India	5,850,000
Sao Paulo	Brazil	5,241,000
Canton	China	5,000,000
Teheran	Iran	5,000,000
Leningrad	U.S.S.R.	4,588,000
Shenyang	China	4,400,000
Rio de Janeiro	Brazil	4,315,000
Bangkok	Thailand	4,300,000

World's Longest Bridge Spans

Name	Location	Length in m.
Humber Estuary	Humber, England	1,410
Verrazano-Narrows	Brooklyn — Staten Is., U.S.A.	1,298
Golden Gate	San Francisco Bay U.S.A.	1,280
Mackinac	Straits of Mackinac, Michigan, U.S.A.	1,158
Atatürk	Bosphorus, Istanbul, Turkey	1,074
George Washington	Hudson River, New York City, U.S.A.	1,067

World's Longest Vehicular Tunnels

Name	Place	Length in km.
Seikan (rail)	Tsugaru Channel, Japan	53.90
Northern Line (tube)	East Finchley—Morden, London	27.84
Simplon (rail)	Brigue, Switzerland, to Iselle, Italy	19.83
Shin-Kanmon (rail)	Kanmon Strait, Japan	18.70
Appenine (rail)	North of Vernio, Italy	18.49
St. Gotthard (road)	Göschenen to Airolo, Switzerland	16.30

Name	Place	Length in km.
Rokko (rail)	Japan	16.0
Henderson (rail)	Rocky Mountains, Colorado, U.S.A.	15.80
St. Gotthard (rail)	Göschenen to Airolo, Switzerland	14.90
Lötschberg (rail)	Kandersteg to Goppenstein, Switzerland	14.50

World's Tallest Buildings

Name	City	No. of storeys	Height in m.
Sears Tower	Chicago	110	443
Empire State Building	New York	102	412
World Trade Centre	New York	110	381
Standard Oil Building	Chicago	80	346
John Hancock Centre	Chicago	100	343
Chrysler Building	New York	77	319
Eiffel Tower	Paris		300
60 Wall Tower	New York	67	289
First Canadian Place	Toronto	72	285
40 Wall Tower	New York	71	282
First National City Corp.	New York	59	279

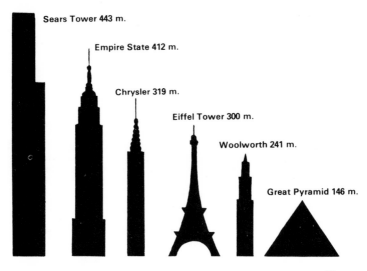

Sears Tower 443 m.

Empire State 412 m.

Chrysler 319 m.

Eiffel Tower 300 m.

Woolworth 241 m.

Great Pyramid 146 m.

Great Britain — Part 1

The British Constitution

The British Constitution is the basis of our form of government and, consequently, our whole way of life. Yet there is no document that lays down the rules of the Constitution — unlike the Constitutions of most other countries — and this gives it a valuable flexibility. The Constitution has grown up over the centuries and it is now universally accepted as the world's most workable form of government.

Parliament — the governing body of the country — has been in existence for 700 years. The first Parliament was summoned by Simon de Montfort in 1265. In the name of the King, he called to Parliament not only the great men of the land, the prelates, earls and barons, but also two elected representatives from every county, city and town. Today, there are two Houses of Parliament, the House of Lords and the House of Commons.

The House of Lords is composed of about 1,100 Lords Spiritual and Temporal. The Lords Spiritual are the Archbishops of Canterbury and York, the Bishops of Lodon, Durham and Winchester and 21 other senior Bishops. The Lords Temporal are the peers and peeresses by descent of England, Scotland, Great Britain or the United Kingdom, new peers, Lords of Appeal in Ordinary (who are life peers) and life peers and life peeresses created under the Life Peerages Act 1958. Under the Peerage Act 1963, a person inheriting a peerage may within one year (or one month in the case of a Member of the House of Commons) disclaim the peerage for life. The right of his heirs to the peerage is not affected.

The House of Commons has a total membership of 635, each member representing one of the 635 parliamentary constituencies of Great Britain. He is elected by the votes of the people.

The Sovereign, as Head of State, has a great number of theoretical powers. He or she makes peace and war, issues charters, creates peers, appoints the Prime Minister, summons or dissolves Parliament, gives the Royal Assent to laws passed by Parliament. In practice, the Sovereign would be unlikely to act against the advice of his or her ministers. In a sense this makes the Monarch little more than a puppet figure but, because he or she is considered to be 'above politics', and cannot in fairness be blamed for the actions of the government, the Royal Family is probably more highly regarded and held in greater affection by the British people today than at any other time in Britain's history.

Legislation

Any ordered community must have laws by which its people may live in peace. Your school has laws — though they are probably called rules — which apply to every member of the school. They were drawn up by your teachers and you know the penalties for breaking them. Similarly, Great Britain, which is a community of more than 55,000,000 people, has laws, and these were formed by Parliament. A new law starts life as a *Bill* and can be introduced either by the Government of the day or by a private Member of Parliament. A bill, except a money bill which must originate in the House of Commons, can be introduced in either House, when it receives its *First Reading*. The next stage is the *Second Reading* when it is debated by the House. If passed, it is referred to a Committee (that is, a Committee of the whole House, a Select Committee, appointed for a specific purpose, or a Standing Committee, which considers public bills). This is called the *Committee Stage,* and the bill is discussed clause by clause before being returned to the House with or without amendment. The next step is the *Report Stage,* when it is either accepted or referred back to the same or another committee. Finally, the bill receives its *Third Reading* and is sent to the other House. Once a bill has been passed by both Houses, it becomes an *Act of Parliament,* provided the Sovereign has given it the *Royal Assent.* The Sovereign is allowed to withhold assent (sometimes called the *Royal Veto*) but this has not happened since 1707, in the reign of Queen Anne.

Political Parties

Most Members of Parliament belong to a political party, whose collective views they normally share. Before a General Election, each party prepares the plans it will carry out should it be given an overall majority by the electorate and thus be able to form a government. These plans are published in what is called a *Manifesto.* Today, most Members of the House of Commons represent a particular party, so that, although the voters may not know a candidate personally, their decision to vote for him depends on whether they like the party he belongs to. Once elected, a Member is expected to follow his party's policies and to vote in the House of Commons according to the party line. This can be very important where a government has only a small majority because a defeat of the government in a vital debate means that the party in power can no longer govern efficiently and the Prime Minister may decide to dissolve Parliament and hold a General Election.

The vote taken at the end of the Parliamentary debate is known as a *Division.* To ensure that its members are present in the House for an important division, each party appoints a few of its members to act as *Whips.* The whips keep members informed of forthcoming debates—usually by means of a circular letter or appeal, which is also known as a 'whip'. For a particularly important debate, the letter will be underlined three times and headed 'Most important'. Failure by the Member to respond to a three-line whip could mean that his party's support is withdrawn from him. At the next election, he could find that he no longer had the financial support of the party.

The Prime Minister

After an election is over and all the votes have been counted, the leader of the party which has gained the largest number of seats is summoned by the Sovereign and invited to form a government. The position of Prime Minister has been in existence since 1721, although it was not officially recognised until 1905. The Prime Minister's chief constitutional duty is to act as a link between the administration and the Crown. He sends all important state documents and correspondence to the Sovereign and advises him or her when to dissolve Parliament. Since 1916, the office has been held by the following:

Name	Government	Took office
D. Lloyd George	Coalition	Dec 7, 1916
A. Bonar Law	Conservative	Oct 23, 1922
S. Baldwin	Conservative	May 22, 1923
J. R. MacDonald	Labour	Jan 22, 1924
S. Baldwin	Conservative	Nov 4, 1924
J. R. MacDonald	Labour	June 8, 1929
J. R. MacDonald	National	Aug 25, 1931
S. Baldwin	National	June 7, 1935
N. Chamberlain	National	May 28, 1937
Winston Churchill	Coalition	May 11, 1940
Winston Churchill	Conservative	May 23, 1945
C. R. Atlee	Labour	July 26, 1945
Sir Winston Churchill	Conservative	Oct 26, 1951
Sir Anthony Eden	Conservative	Apr 6, 1955
Harold Macmillan	Conservative	Jan 13, 1957
Sir Alec Douglas-Home	Conservative	Oct 19, 1963
Harold Wilson	Labour	Oct 16, 1964
Edward Heath	Conservative	June 24, 1970
Harold Wilson	Labour	Mar 4, 1974
James Callaghan	Labour	April 5, 1976
Margaret Thatcher	Conservative	May 17, 1979

Houses of Parliament

Kings and Queens of England (since A.D. 927)

Before the year 927, England was composed of nine separate little kingdoms, Kent, South Saxons, West Saxons, Bernicia, Northumbria, Mercia, Deira, East Angles, East Saxons. King Athelstan, grandson of King Alfred of the West Saxons, was the first to establish rule over all England, which he did in 927. This overall rule was lost from time to time in succeeding years.

Name	Parents	Married	Came to throne	Length of reign	Died
Athelstan b. 895	Edward the Elder and Queen Egwyn	—	925	15 yrs.	940
Edmund b 921	Edward the Elder and Queen Eadgifu	1. Elgifu 2. Ethelfled	940	6 yrs.	age 45 946
Edred b. 923	Edward the Elder and Queen Eadgifu	—	946	9 yrs.	age 25 955
Edwy b. 941	King Edmund and Queen Elgifu	—	955	4 yrs.	age 32 959
Edgar b. 943	King Edmund and Queen Elgifu	1. Ethelfled 2. Elfthryth	959	16 yrs.	age 18 975
Edward the Martyr b. 963	King Edgar and Queen Ethelfled	—	975	3 yrs.	age 32 978
Ethelred II (The Unready) b. 968	King Edgar and Queen Elfthryth	1. Elfgifu 2. Emma, dau. of Duke of Normandy	978	37 yrs.	age 17 1016
Edmund Ironside b. 989	King Ethelred II and Queen Elfgifu	—	1016	6 mths.	age 48 1016
Canute the Dane b. 995	King Swegn Forkbeard of Denmark. Took throne by force	1. Elfgifu 2. Emma, widow of Ethelred	1017	18 yrs.	age 27 1035 age 40

Name	Parents	Married	Came to throne	Length of reign	Died
Harold I b. 1016?	King Canute and Queen Elfgifu	—	1035	5 yrs.	1040 age 24
Hardicanute b.1018	King Canute and Queen Emma	—	1040	2 yrs.	1042 age 24
Edward The Confessor b. 1004	King Ethelred II and Queen Emma	1. Emma, dau. of Earl Godwin	1042	24 yrs.	1066 age 62
Harold II b. 1022	Earl Godwin Brother of Queen Emma	—	1066	10 mths.	1066 age 44
The House of Normandy					
William I b. 1027	Duke of Normandy Took throne by conquest	Matilda, dau. of Count of Flanders	1066	21 yrs.	1087 age 60
William II b. 1057	King William I and Queen Matilda	Unmarried	1087	13 yrs.	1100 age 43
Henry I b. 1068	King William I and Queen Matilda	1. Matilda of Scotland 2. Adelicia	1100	35 yrs.	1135 age 67
Stephen b. 1104	Count of Blois Grandson of King William I	Matilda, dau. of Count of Boulogne	1135	19 yrs.	1154 age 50
The House of Plantagenet					
Henry II b. 1133	Geoffrey Plantagenet Grandson of King Henry I	Eleanor, dau. of Duke of Guienne	1154	35 yrs.	1189 age 56
Richard I b. 1157	King Henry II and Queen Eleanor	Berengaria, dau. of King of Navarre	1189	10 yrs.	1199 age 42

Name	Parents	Married	Came to throne	Length of reign	Died
John b. 1167	King Henry II and Queen Eleanor	1. Avisa, dau. of Earl of Gloucester 2. Isabella, dau. of Count of Angoulême	1199	17 yrs.	1216 age 49
Henry III b. 1207	King John and Queen Isabella	Eleanor, dau. of Count of Provence	1216	56 yrs.	1272 age 65
Edward I b. 1239	King Henry III and Queen Eleanor	1. Eleanor of Castile 2. Margaret of France	1272	35 yrs.	1307 age 68
Edward II b. 1284	King Edward I and Queen Eleanor	Isabella, dau. of Philip of France	1307	20 yrs.	1327 age 43
Edward III b. 1312	King Edward II and Queen Isabella	Philippa, dau. of Count of Holland and Hainault	1327	50 yrs.	1377 age 65
Richard II b. 1367	The Black Prince Grandson of King Edward III	1. Anne of Bohemia 2. Isabel of France	1377	22 yrs.	Deposed 1399 Died 1400 age 33
The House of Lancaster					
Henry IV b. 1366	John of Gaunt Grandson of King Edward III	1. Mary of Bohun 2. Johanna of Navarre	1399	13 yrs.	1413 age 47
Henry V b. 1388	King Henry IV and Lady Mary of Bohun	Katherine of France	1413	9 yrs.	1422 age 34

Name	Parents	Married	Came to throne	Length of reign	Died
Henry VI b. 1421	King Henry V and Queen Katherine	Margaret of Anjou	1422	39 yrs.	Deposed 1461 Died 1471 age 49
The House of York					
Edward IV b. 1442	Richard, Duke of York Great-great-grandson of King Edward III	Elizabeth, dau. of Sir Richard Woodville	1461	22 yrs.	1483 age 41
Edward V b. 1470	King Edward IV and Queen Elizabeth	Unmarried	1483	About 3 mths.	1483 age 13
Richard III b. 1452	Richard, Duke of York Brother of King Edward IV	Anne, dau. of Earl of Warwick	1483	2 yrs.	1485 age 33
The House of Tudor					
Henry VII b. 1457	Grandson of Owen Tudor and Katherine, widow of Henry V	Elizabeth, dau. of King Edward IV	1485	24 yrs.	1509 age 53
Henry VIII b. 1491	King Henry VII and Queen Elizabeth of Aragon (Div.)	1. Katherine of Aragon (Div.) 2. Anne Boleyn (Beheaded) 3. Jane Seymour (Died) 4. Anne of Cleves (Divorced)	1509	38 yrs.	1547 age 56

Name	Parents	Married	Came to throne	Length of reign	Died
		5. Katherine Howard (Beheaded) 6. Katherine Parr			
Edward VI b. 1537	King Henry VIII and Jane Seymour	Unmarried	1547	6 yrs.	1553 age 16
Lady Jane Grey b. 1537	Marquess of Dorset Great-niece of Henry VIII	Lord Guildford Dudley	1553	14 days	1554 age 17
Mary I b. 1516	King Henry VIII and Katherine of Aragon	Philip of Spain	1553	5 yrs.	1558
Elizabeth I b. 1533	King Henry VIII and Anne Boleyn	Unmarried	1558	44 yrs.	1603 age 69
The House of Stuart					
James I b. 1566	Mary, Queen of Scots, Great-great-grandson of King Henry VII	Anne of Denmark	1603	22 yrs.	1625 age 59
Charles I b. 1600	King James I and Queen Anne	Henrietta-Maria of France	1625	24 yrs.	1649 age 48
Charles II b. 1630	King Charles I and Queen Henrietta-Maria	Catherine of Braganza	1649 (Restored 1660)	36 yrs.	1685 age 55

(Note: Commonwealth declared 1649 after Charles I's execution. Oliver Cromwell, Lord Protector, 1653-1658; Richard Cromwell, Lord Protector, 1658-1659).

Name	Parents	Married	Came to throne	Length of reign	Died
James II	King Charles I and	1. Lady Anne Hyde	1685	3 yrs.	Deposed

Name	Parents	Married	Came to throne	Length of reign	Died
b. 1633	Queen Henrietta-Maria	2. Mary of Modena			1688 Died 1701 age 68
William III b. 1650 and	William of Orange		Jointly 1689	13 yrs.	1702 age 51
Mary II b. 1662	King James and Lady Anne Hyde			6 yrs.	1694 age 33
Anne b. 1665	King James II and Lady Anne Hyde	Prince George of Denmark	1702	12 yrs.	1714 age 49
The House of Hanover					
George I b. 1660	Elector of Hanover and Sophia (grand-dau. of James I)	Sophia of Zell	1714	13 yrs.	1727 age 67
George II b. 1683	King George I and Sophia of Zell	Caroline of Brandenburg-Auspach	1727	33 yrs.	1760 age 77
George III b. 1738	Frederick, Prince of Wales Grandson of King George II	Charlotte of Mecklenburg-Strelitz	1760	59 yrs.	1820 age 81
George IV b. 1762	King George III and Queen Charlotte	1. Mary Anne Fitzherbert 2. Caroline of Brunswick-Wolfenbüttel	1820	10 yrs.	1830 age 67

Name	Parents	Married	Came to throne	Length of reign	Died
William IV b. 1765	King George III and Queen Charlotte Duke of Kent	Adelaide of Saxe-Meiningen	1830	7 yrs.	1837 age 71
Victoria b. 1819	Grand-daughter of George III	Albert of Saxe-Coburg and Gotha	1837	63 yrs.	1901 age 81
The House of Saxe-Coburg					
Edward VII b. 1841	Queen Victoria and Prince Albert	Princess Alexandra of Denmark	1901	9 yrs.	1910 age 68
The House of Windsor					
George V b. 1865	King Edward VII and Queen Alexandra	Princess Mary of Teck	1910	25 yrs.	1936 age 70
Edward VIII b. 1894	King George V and Queen Mary	Mrs. Wallis Simpson	1936	325 days	Abdicated 1936
George VI b. 1895	King George V and Queen Mary	The Lady Elizabeth Angela Marguerite, dau. of the 14th Earl of Strathmore and Kinghorne (H.M. Queen Elizabeth the Queen Mother)	1936	15 yrs.	1952 age 56
Elizabeth II b. 1926	King George VI and Queen Elizabeth	Philip, son of Prince Andrew of Greece (H.R.H. the Duke of Edinburgh)	1952	—	—

Great Britain — Part 2

Local Government in Great Britain
England and Wales

Local administration is carried out by four different types of bodies: (i) local branches of some central ministries, such as the Ministry of Social Security; (ii) local sub-managements of nationalised industries (coal, electricity, gas, public transport and the Post Office); (iii) specialist authorities such as the police and water conservation; and (iv) the system of *local government*. The Local Government Act of 1972 created a new system which took effect from April, 1974.

England and Wales have somewhat different systems. Each country has 3 types of council in common, i.e. *county, district* and English *parish* or Welsh *community* councils. In addition, England has some *metropolitan* county and district councils. Councillors are elected by their local electors for 4 years. A district may be granted the honorific status of a 'Borough' and a parish or community council may call itself a 'Town' Council. The president of a borough council is called the Mayor, or in a few famous places, the Lord Mayor. The others are called chairmen. They are elected annually by their councils.

There are 47 non-metropolitan counties (eight are in Wales) and six metropolitan counties. Within the counties there are 347 districts (36 metropolitan, and 311 non-metropolitan, of which 37 districts are in Wales).

The English districts consist of about 10,000 Parishes and some 500 areas which are not parishes. About 7,000 of the parishes have councils. The Welsh districts are divided into about 1,000 communities, some 800 of which have councils.

County boundaries were laid down by the Local Government Act, 1972, and the district boundaries were settled by orders made in 1973 under that Act.

Local government functions may be classified into county, district and sub-district functions. For example, *county functions* include the formulation of development plans, traffic, transportation and roads, education, public libraries and museums, youth employment and social services.

Greater London

Since 1965, the Metropolitan area, with a population of 6.92 million has had a Greater London Council (GLC) and has been divided into 32 London Boroughs. The City is in most respects independent of the surrounding system, and has an ancient constitution.

England, Non-Metropolitan Counties

Name	Population	Area in hectares	Admin. Offices
Avon	920,600	133,956	Bristol
Bedfordshire	505,250	123,444	Bedford
Berkshire	694,200	124,314	Reading
Buckinghamshire	541,000	187,781	Aylesbury
Cambridgeshire	600,760	340,933	Cambridge
Cheshire	930,800	232,231	Chester
Cleveland	571,200	58,311	Middlesbrough
Cornwall	422,000	354,636	Truro
Cumbria	472,000	680,802	Carlisle
Derbyshire	907,500	263,092	Matlock
Devonshire	956,800	652,507	Exeter
Dorset	593,600	230,441	Dorchester
Durham	604,400	243,620	Durham
Essex	1,457,700	367,406	Chelmsford
Gloucestershire	499,700	264,164	Gloucester
Hampshire	1,461,300	386,488	Winchester
Hereford & Worcester	624,290	392,559	Worcester
Hertfordshire	953,500	163,424	Hertford
Humberside	848,000	351,192	Beverley
Isle of Wight	116,000	38,096	Newport
Kent	1,456,800	372,998	Maidstone
Lancashire	1,388,100	300,465	Preston
Leicestershire	845,500	255,305	Leicester
Lincolnshire	540,600	588,544	Lincoln
Norfolk	1,323,371	956,266	Norwich
Northamptonshire	689,800	236,753	Northampton
Northumberland	287,400	410,800	Newcastle upon Tyne
Nottinghamshire	984,300	210,831	Nottingham
Oxfordshire	550,100	261,158	Oxford
Salop	376,000	349,048	Shrewsbury
Somerset	414,700	345,795	Taunton
Staffordshire	1,001,900	265,969	Stafford
Suffolk	602,900	380,742	Ipswich
Surrey	988,500	165,465	Kingston-upon-Thames
Sussex, East	656,000	179,536	Lewes
Sussex, West	648,900	201,670	Chichester
Warwickshire	476,500	198,020	Warwick
Wiltshire	521,700	348,082	Trowbridge
Yorkshire, North	667,400	831,658	Northallerton

Metropolitan Counties, England

Name	Population	Area in hectares	Admin. Offices
Greater Manchester	2,645,000	128,430	Manchester
Merseyside	1,521,000	64,752	Liverpool

Name	Population	Area in hectares	Admin. Offices
Tyne & Wear	1,158,575	53,982	Newcastle upon Tyne
West Midlands	2,655,800	89,948	Birmingham
Yorkshire, South	1,295,600	156,117	Barnsley
Yorkshire, West	2,067,000	203,913	Wakefield

Wales

Name	Population	Area in hectares	Admin. Offices
Clwyd	382,530	242,415	Mold
Dyfed	325,600	576,697	Carmarthen
Gwent	435,600	137,742	Cwmbran
Gwynedd	228,000	386,488	Caernarvon
Mid Glamorgan	541,700	101,876	Cardiff
Powys	108,400	507,898	Llandrindod Wells
South Glamorgan	396,900	41,606	Cardiff
West Glamorgan	364,900	81,537	Swansea

Scotland

In May, 1975, local government in Scotland was reorganised. There are now nine mainland regions and three island councils.

Region	Population	Area in hectares	Admin. Offices
Borders	99,938	467,124	Newton St. Boswells
Central	271,177	251,747	Stirling
Dumfries & Galloway	142,547	637,138	Dumfries
Fife	340,176	130,536	Glenrothes
Grampian	469,168	870,398	Aberdeen
Highland	190,507	2,541,558	Inverness
Lothian	750,728	175,601	Edinburgh
Orkney	18,134	97,468	Kirkwall
Shetland	21,835	142,586	Lerwick
Strathclyde	2,445,283	3,422,520	Glasgow
Tayside	401,987	766,507	Dundee
Western Isles	30,691	290,079	Stornoway, Lewis

Northern Ireland, District and Borough Councils

On October 1, 1973, the County Councils were replaced by 26 District and Borough Councils.

Name	Population	Area in hectares	Admin. Offices
Antrim	40,000	56,253	Antrim
Ards	53,200	36,132	Newtownards
Armagh	47,500	67,461	Armagh
Ballymena	53,200	41,785	Ballymena
Ballymoney	22,000	41,785	Ballymoney

Name	Population	Area in hectares	Admin. Offices
Banbridge	28,800	44,530	Banbridge
Belfast City	354,400	11,516	Belfast
Carrickfergus	27,900	7,696	Carrickfergus
Castlereagh	63,900	8,445	Belfast
Coleraine	45,500	48,445	Coleraine
Cookstown	27,900	61,086	Cookstown
Craigavon	73,100	38,821	Lurgan, Portadown
Down	48,800	65,427	Downpatrick
Dungannon	42,300	33,517	Dungannon
Fermanagh	50,900	185,100	Enniskillen
Larne	28,400	33,988	Larne
Limavady	25,600	62,162	Limavady
Lisburn	82,300	44,377	Lisburn
Londonderry City	87,900	38,346	Londonderry
Magherafelt	32,300	63,538	Magherafelt
Moyle	13,000	49,407	Ballycastle
Newry & Mourne	76,100	90,957	Newry
Newtownabbey	75,000	13,005	Newtownabbey
North Down	61,500	7,679	Bangor
Omagh	41,700	112,498	Omagh
Strabane	35,600	86,156	Strabane

Principal British Cities

Name	Population	Name	Population
Greater London	6,970,000	Belfast	354,000
Birmingham	1,041,000	Coventry	340,000
Glasgow	809,000	Wakefield	308,000
Leeds	728,500	Salford	291,000
Sheffield	544,000	Newcastle upon Tyne	289,000
Liverpool	537,000	Kingston-upon-Hull	286,000
Manchester	488,500	Nottingham	283,000
Bradford	465,000	Cardiff	279,000
Edinburgh	455,000	Leicester	277,500
Bristol	410,000	Plymouth	260,300

Highest Peaks

Scotland

Ben Nevis, Inverness	1,343 m.
Ben Macdhui, Aberdeenshire	1,309 m.
Braeriach, Aberdeenshire	1,295 m.
Cairn Toul, Aberdeenshire	1,293 m.

Wales

Snowdon, Gwynedd	1,085 m.
Carnedd, Llewellyn, Gwynedd	1,062 m.
Carnedd Dafydd, Gwynedd	1,044 m.

Highest Peaks

Wales
Glyder Fawr, Gwynedd   999 m.
England
Scafell Pike, Cumbria   978 m.
Sca Fell, Cumbria   964 m.
Hellvellyn, Cumbria   950 m.
Skiddaw, Cumbria   930 m.

Longest Rivers

Name	Mouth	Length (km.)
Severn	Bristol Channel	354
Thames	North Sea	338
Trent-Humber	North Sea	298
Aire-Ouse-Humber	North Sea	259
Ouse (Great)	The Wash	230
Wye	River Severn	217
Tay-Tummel	North Sea	188
Nene	The Wash	161
Clyde	Atlantic Ocean	158.5
Spey	North Sea	157.7

The Cinque Ports

Though the word, 'Cinque', comes from the French and means five, it is pronounced 'sink'. Originally, there were five of these ports, part of the Anglo-Saxon system (inherited from the Romans) of coastal defence between the Wash and Spithead. The five original Cinque Ports are Hastings, New Romney, Hythe, Dover and Sandwich. Some time after the Norman Conquest, two further ports were added to the group — Winchelsea and Rye. Lydd, Faversham, Folkestone, Deal, Tenterden, Margate and Ramsgate also belong to the Confederation of Cinque Ports and are known as Limbs. The present Lord Warden of the Cinque Ports is H.M. Queen Elizabeth the Queen Mother, who succeeded the Rt. Hon. Sir Robert Menzies in 1978.

Highway Code

Anyone taking a driving test will be examined on his knowledge of the Highway Code. Pedestrians, cyclists and riders of horses do not have to pass a test in order to use a road, but it is just as important for them to study the Highway Code and remember the rules it lays down.

Pedestrians

1. Where there is a pavement or footpath, use it.
2. Do not walk next to the kerb with your back to the oncoming traffic. Look first before stepping off the pavement.
3. Where there is no footpath, walk on the right-hand side of the road to face oncoming traffic.
4. Do not linger in the roadway or walk along cycle tracks.

5. Use subways, footbridges, pedestrian crossings or centre islands when crossing the road.

6. You have right of way on a zebra crossing, but always allow oncoming vehicles plenty of time to stop, especially when the road is wet or icy. Do not stand at a zebra crossing if you do not intend to cross. Where a zebra crossing has a centre island, treat each half as a separate crossing.

7. If traffic lights have 'CROSS NOW' signal, do not cross until the signal appears.

8. Do not cross the road against a signal to stop by a policeman controlling the traffic.

9. Do not get off a bus except at the recognised bus-stops.

Pedal Cyclists

1. If there is a special cycle track, use it.

2. In company, never ride more than two abreast. If the traffic in the road is heavy, ride in single file.

3. Never carry anything that may interfere with your control of the bicycle.

4. Do not hold on to a moving vehicle or another cyclist.

5. Do not ride close behind a moving vehicle.

By law you must:

1. See that your cycle has efficient brakes.

2. Observe traffic signs and signals and the directions of a policeman controlling traffic.

3. Stop when signalled to do so by a School Crossing Patrol.

4. Stop for pedestrians waiting to cross the road by a zebra crossing.

5. Stop for pedestrians at a panda crossing when the flashing amber light is showing.

6. See that, at night, your front and rear lamps are alight and that your cycle has an efficient red reflector.

7. Keep to the nearside edge of the road when wheeling your cycle along the road at night without lights.

8. Stop when asked to do so by a policeman in uniform.

I am turning left

I am turning right

Signs Giving Orders

No entry

No right turn

No left turn

School crossing ahead

Stop and give way

Give way to traffic on major road

Turn left ahead (right if symbol reversed)

Turn left (right if symbol reversed)

No cycling or moped-riding

All vehicles prohibited

Route for cyclists and moped riders (compulsory)

BLACK

BLUE

RED

Ahead only

Plate supplementing 'Turn' signs

Keep left (right if symbol reversed)

Pass
either
side

Warning Signs

Steep hill downwards

Steep hill upwards

Pedestrian crossing

Road works

Level crossing without barrier ahead

Uneven road

Slippery road

Danger: plate indicates nature of danger

Information Signs

Cyclists and moped-riders only

41

Traffic Light Signals

Accidents can be caused by a misunderstanding of traffic lights. Study the drawings and remember the instructions.

Red means stop. Wait behind the stop-line on the roadway.

Red and **Amber** together also mean stop. Do not go on until the green light shows.

Green means you may go on IF the road is clear. If you are turning left or right, give way to pedestrians who are crossing.

 RED

 AMBER

 GREEN

Amber alone means stop at the stop-line. You may only go on if you have passed the stop-line when the light appears.

Green Arrow means that you may go in the direction shown by the arrow, whatever other lights may be showing.

42

Europe and the EEC

The European Economic Community (EEC)
The European Economic Community was brought into being by the Treaty of Rome, signed on March 25, 1957 by France, Germany, Italy, Belgium, the Netherlands and Luxembourg. In 1972, the British Parliament approved a decision that Britain should join on terms which had been negotiated. Denmark and Ireland joined at the same time as Britain, in January, 1973, increasing the EEC membership to nine. Britain's membership was confirmed by a national referendum held in June, 1975. Greece became the tenth member in 1981. Portugal and Spain have formally applied to join the Community.

Aims and Objectives
While one of the aims of the Community is to promote closer union among the people of Europe, member states retain their own national institutions. Other objectives include economic and social progress with improved living and working conditions for its peoples; trade restrictions are to be abolished.

Achievements
There are now no customs duties on goods bought from other member states, but imports from the rest of the world are subject to a common tariff. Measures have been taken to free the movement of capital and for the nationals of any member country to seek or take up work in any of the others. Here are common policies for agriculture, energy and transport, and special loans and grants available for economic assistance.

Organisation and Government
A Council of Ministers represent the governments of the member states, one minister for each country (10). The ministers make important Community decisions and regulations binding on all other member states. What has been agreed is enforced by an executive body, the Commission, representing the Community as a whole. The Commission has 14 permanent members: two each from Britain, France, Germany and Italy; and one from each of the other member countries. Not only are directives and authorisations sent out to member countries but non-binding opinions given. Proposals also are made to the Council. Community disputes are settled by the European Court of Justice. The total number of M.P.'s in the European Parliament is now 434.

The Common Market
The term 'Common Market' embraces not only the European Economic Community but the European Coal and Steel Community (established 1951) and the European Atomic Energy Community (EURATOM).

The European Free Trade Association (EFTA)

EFTA was established on March 27, 1961. It was formed by seven nations: Great Britain; Austria; Denmark; Norway; Portugal; Sweden; and Switzerland. Between them, tariffs were abolished on industrial goods. Later, Finland joined as an associate member and Iceland as a full member. Britain and Denmark left EFTA on joining the EEC. The remaining countries signed a free trade agreement with the EEC on July 22, 1972; Norway signed on May 14, 1973.

SCHOOL SYSTEMS

Great Britain

In G.B. schooling is compulsory for all children between the ages five and 16 years. Many stay on at school after the minimum leaving age. British schools are maintained either by local authorities or (a small percentage) are independent. About eighty per cent of maintained schools are co-educational. There are two types of maintained school: county schools, built, maintained and staffed by local authorities; and voluntary schools, built mainly by religious denominations but maintained by a local authority.

State Schools

Education under the state system is usually in two stages, primary and secondary. Primary schools are normally for children aged five to 11; most take both boys and girls. But, however, there are some schools for children up to the age of seven only, and others for juniors aged seven to 11. In some areas there are so-called first schools which take pupils of ages five to eight, nine or ten. These children then go on to middle schools which cover age ranges from eight to 14. More middle schools are planned as local authorities introduce a three-tier system of comprehensive education to replace the two-tier traditional system.

Secondary schools are for children aged 11 to 16 and over. There are four main types of secondary school. Comprehensive schools admit pupils without any reference to ability. Some of these schools are very large with over 2,000 pupils. Secondary modern schools provide a general education with a leaning towards practical subjects. Grammar schools provide a more academic education for pupils aged 11 to 18. There are also a small number of technical schools which provide a course that combines academic and technical studies.

Independent Schools

Independent schools charge fees and do not receive grants from public funds. At the secondary level most independent schools are for either boys or girls only. The term public school denotes independent schools, principally boarding schools for children of 12 to 18 years, whose heads are members of the Headmasters' Conference or the Governing Bodies Association. Preparatory schools are mainly for boys from the ages of about eight to 13 years who wish to enter public schools.

Examination Systems

Children at secondary schools can take the General Certificate of Education (G.C.E.) examination which is set at two levels, Ordinary level and Advanced level. Ordinary ('O') level is usually taken at the age of 16 and Advanced ('A') level two years later. Candidates may sit for one or more subjects as they wish. The Certificate of Secondary Education (C.S.E.) can also be taken in one or more subjects. This examination is open to any boy or girl who has completed five years of secondary education. The Government has plans to replace the G.C.E. 'O' levels and C.S.E. examinations by a single system.

France

Schooling is compulsory between the ages of six and 16. About twenty per cent of French schools are private, these being chiefly run by the Catholic church.

At state schools the educational stages are as follows. Children aged six to 11 are given elementary instruction at primary schools. There is a common curriculum divided into successive levels. Wednesday is always a day off, but children have to go to school on Saturdays.

After primary school all children receive a secondary education at schools called *collèges*, where a balanced range of subjects is taught, providing a foundation for the subsequent education or vocational training. There is a common curriculum and schooling falls into two two-year cycles. During the first cycle all pupils have 24 hours a week of: French, mathematics, a foreign language, history, geography, civics, experimental sciences, artistic subjects, physical education and sport. The same subjects are studied in the second cycle but in addition three further hours must be given to one of the following subjects: Latin, Greek, second modern language, or technology. At the end of the second cycle a certificate is awarded on the strength of the pupil's work during the year or by examination.

After *collège*, secondary schooling for most children is continued in the *lycées*, from the age of 15. *Lycées* prepare pupils in three years for one of three examinations: *baccalauréat* of secondary education, technical baccalauréat, or *brevet de technician.* These are the gateways to university or technical institutes.

Children aged 14 on completing the first cycle at *collège* who want to embark on pre-vocational studies çan attend preparatory classes, either in the *collèges*, or in *lycées d'enseignment professionel* (schools for vocational instruction).

Italy

Education is compulsory for all children from six to 14 years of age. Primary schooling lasts for five years, followed by three years at junior secondary school. There are several kinds of senior secondary school, for pupils of 14 years upwards. An education with an emphasis on classical languages is given at a *ginnasio* for children aged 14 to 16. This is continued at a *liceo* for another three years. Pupils with a scientific bent might elect to go to a scientific *liceo*. There are also schools with an emphasis on modern languages. Various kinds of technical school offer five year courses in special subjects at the end of which the pupil is ready, at the age of 19, to enter a profession, such as accountancy, surveying and primary school teaching. All Italian schoolchildren take an examination called the *Licenza* at the age of 14. At the age of 19 an advanced examination is taken, the *Maturità*, which is the gateway to university.

West Germany

German children start school at the age of six. The minimum leaving age is 15. The first or primary school (*grundschule*) is attended for four years. A child may then attend a post-primary school (*Hauptschule*). Or, according to ability, he may go to a *Realschule* or *Gymnasium* (grammar school). At the *Realschule* practical subjects such as shorthand and typing are included in the curriculum to prepare children for careers in the world of business. Pupils attend the *Realschule* for six years. The academically inclined would attend a *Gymnasium*, of which there are two kinds. One, the *humanistische gymnasium*, includes classical languages among the subjects taught. The other, the *neuspratchliche* (new language) *gymnasium* puts an emphasis on modern languages and the sciences. Children attend the *Gymnasium* for nine years at the end of which they take an examination called the *Abitur*. Comprehensive schools have been introduced in some German states.

School Holidays

Great Britain
In the U.K. the number of days a state school has to meet in a year is set at 200 by Act of Parliament. However, a school can meet up to ten days fewer than 200 days for so-called 'occasional' holidays (for special occasions). Local authorities determine what the holiday dates will be. Generally speaking, schools have three weeks at Easter, six weeks in the summer and three weeks at Christmas. In addition there is a holiday lasting about one week at half term. To cut fuel costs, some local education authorities are now extending the Christmas holiday from three to four weeks, but a week is knocked off the summer holiday to compensate. Independent schools are free to arrange holidays as they choose.

Europe
Holiday dates are less variable in some European countries. In *Germany* the dates are fixed by the ministry for education. They are staggered between the different German states, however. For example, in one year, say in Hessen, the summer holiday might begin on June 18th and end on July 31st. Bavaria might not start the summer holidays until July 29th and end on September 13th. In general, German schoolchildren have about two weeks off for Easter, a short break for Whitsun, six weeks for summer, a week's holiday in autumn and two to three weeks at Christmas.

In *Italy*, too, holidays are decided by the ministry of education, in Rome. School holidays are the same everywhere. The school year starts about

September 15th and ends about June 15th. There are breaks of about ten days for Christmas and five for Easter. There are no half-term holidays.

School holidays in *France* are now decided by the central ministry. Many French children and their parents like to go skiing in the holidays, but ski resorts would be swamped if all schools were on holiday at the same time. Accordingly, the various regions of the country are given different holiday dates. There is generally two weeks for the Christmas and spring (Easter) holidays, and eight weeks in the summer. In addition there are half-term holidays lasting about a week each term.

The Christian Festivals

Easter Day can fall on any Sunday between March 22nd and April 25th, being determined by the lunar cycle. However, the World Council of Churches is trying to obtain a unanimous choice of a fixed date for Easter. Unless the date is fixed, Easter and other movable feasts will fall as shown in the table below.

	Ash Wednesday	Easter	Ascension	Whit Sunday	Advent
1982	Feb. 24	Apr. 11	May 20	May 30	Nov. 28
1983	Feb. 16	Apr. 3	May 12	May 22	Nov. 27
1984	Mar. 7	Apr. 22	May 31	Jun 10	Dec. 2
1985	Feb. 20	Apr. 7	May 16	May 26	Dec. 1
1986	Feb. 12	Mar. 30	May 8	May 18	Nov. 10

Ash Wednesday is the first day of Lent—which ends at midnight before Easter Day. Lent is a period of 40 days during which many Christians try to give up something they enjoy—such as sweets.

Ascension Day commemorates Christ's ascension into heaven. It is the 40th day after Easter, falling on a Thursday.

Whit Sunday is a festival held seven weeks after Easter and corresponds to the Jewish Pentecost. It commemorates the descent of the Holy Spirit on the apostles.

Advent Sunday is the nearest Sunday (before or after) to St. Andrew's Day (November 30th). The period of Advent is a preparation for Christmas.

Trinity Sunday is the Sunday after Whit Sunday.

Corpus Christi falls on the Thursday following Trinity Sunday.

Epiphany falls on the 6th January. The Twelfth Night of Christmas, the visit of the Magi to the infant Jesus is commemorated.

All Saints Day (November 1st) is a celebration in honour of saints known and unknown. It is a day when Christians are expected to attend Communion service.

All Soul's Day (November 2nd) is when the church specially remembers all who have died. Also known as All Hallow's Day, it had been the Celtic New Year.

Secular Holidays

New Year's Day (January 1st)—of Roman origin.

May Day (May 1st) probably stems from the Roman festival to Maia, mother of Mercury and for centuries the first day of her month was a time for considerable merry-making. In modern times May 1st has been designated Labour Day — the day of the working people.

European Public Holidays

Many public holidays are days of religious significance. Some are of pagan origin. Others are days of special importance to a particular nation, marking a political or historical event.

Great Britain Jan. 1; March 17 (St. Patrick's Day) (N. Ireland); Good Friday; Easter Monday (except Scotland); May 1; Whit Monday; July 12 (Orangemen's Day)(N. Ireland); August 2 (Scotland); last Monday in August (not Scotland); Dec. 25; Dec. 26 (unless it falls on a Sunday, when Boxing Day will be on December 27).

Belgium Jan. 1; Easter Monday; May 1; Ascension; Whit Monday; July 21 (National Feast Day); August 15 (Ascension of the Virgin Mary); Nov. 1 (All Saints); Nov. 11 (Armistice Day); Dec. 25.

Denmark Jan. 1; Good Friday, and preceding day; May 7 (General Prayer Day); Ascension; Whit Monday, June 5 (Constitution Day); Dec. 25; 26.

Finland Jan. 1; Epiphany; Good Friday, Easter Sunday and Monday; May 1; Ascension; Whitsun; June 26 (Midsummer Day); Nov. 1; Day; Dec. 6 (Independence Day); Dec. 25; Dec. 26.

France Jan. 1; Easter Monday; May 1; Ascension; Whit Monday; July 14 (Bastille Day); August 15 (Ascension of the Virgin Mary); Nov. 1; Nov. 11 (Memorial Day); Dec. 25.

W. Germany Jan. 1; 6 (Baden-Württemburg, Bavaria); Good Friday; Easter Monday; May 1, Ascension; Whit Monday; Corpus Christi (Baden-Württemburg, Hesse, Saarland, Nrd. Rh.-Westf., Rh.-Pfalz, Bavaria); June 17; Aug. 15 (Ascension of the Virgin Mary) (Saarland, Bavaria); Nov. 1 (all except Hesse); Dec. 25; Dec. 26.

Greece Jan. 1; 6; first day of Lent; Mar. 25 (Independence from the Turks); Good Friday, Easter Sunday and Monday (Greek Orthodox); May 1; Whit Monday (Greek Orthodox); Aug. 15 (Ascension of Virgin Mary); Oct. 28 ('No'-Day-day Mussolini's ultimatum was refused); Dec. 25; Dec. 26.

Iceland Jan. 1, Good Friday and preceding day; Easter Sunday and Monday; Apr. 22 (first day of summer); May 1; Ascension; Whit Monday; June 17 (National Day); August 2; Dec. 25; Dec. 26; Dec. 31.

Repub. Ireland Jan. 1; Mar. 17 (St. Patrick's Day); Good Friday; Easter Monday; first Monday in June (spring holiday); Aug. 2; last Monday in October; Dec. 25, 26, 27.

Italy Jan. 1; Easter Monday; Apr. 25 (Liberation Day); Nov. 1; Dec. 8 (Immaculate Conception); Dec. 25; Dec. 26.

Luxembourg Jan. 1; Easter Monday; May 1; Ascension; Whit Monday; June 23 (National Day); Aug. 15 (Ascension of the Virgin Mary); Nov. 1; Dec. 25; Dec. 26.

Monaco Jan. 1; Jan. 27 (feast day of St. Devote); Good Friday; Easter Monday; May 1; Ascension; Whit Monday; Corpus Christi; Aug. 15 (Ascension of the Virgin Mary); Nov. 1; Nov. 18, 19 (National Feast); Dec. 8 (Immaculate Conception); Dec. 25.

Netherlands Jan 1; Good Friday; Easter Monday; Apr. 30; May 5 (Liberation Day); Ascension; Whit Monday; Dec. 25; Dec. 26.

Norway Jan. 1; Good Friday and the day preceding it; Easter Monday; May 17 (National Independence Day); Whit Monday; Dec. 25; Dec. 26.

Portugal Jan. 1; Good Friday; Apr. 25 (Liberation in 1974); May 1; Corpus Christi; June 13 (St. Anthony); Aug. 15 (Ascension of the Virgin Mary); Oct. 5 (Proclamation of the Republic); Nov. 1; Dec. 1 (Restoration of Independence); Dec. 8 (Immaculate Conception).

Spain Jan. 1; Jan. 6; Jan. 22 (Valencia); Mar. 19 (St. Joseph); Good Friday and the following Saturday; Easter Monday (Barcelona); May 1; May 15 (St. Isidro) (Madrid); Corpus Christi; July 25 (St. Joseph, patron saint of Spain); July 31 (Bilbao); Aug. 15 (Ascension of the Virgin Mary); Sept. 24 (Barcelona); Oct. 12 (National Day); Nov. 9 (Madrid); Dec. 8 (Immaculate Conception); Dec. 25; Dec. 26.

Sweden Jan. 1; Jan. 6; Good Friday; Easter Monday; May 1; Ascension; Whit Monday; June 26 (Midsummer Day); Nov. 6; Dec. 25; Dec. 26.

Switzerland Jan. 1, 2; Good Friday; Easter Monday; May 1; Ascension; Whit Monday; Aug. 1 (Swiss National Holiday — afternoon only); Dec. 25.

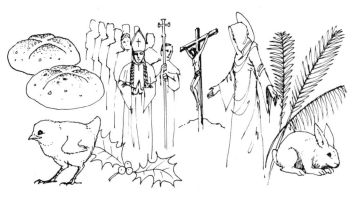

The English Language

Parts of Speech

There are eight parts of speech, dependent on how a word is used in a sentence. They are:

Nouns — denoting persons or things. Proper nouns, such as the names of people or cities, take capital letters.

Adjectives — words used to describe nouns (colour, size, etc.)

Pronouns — these are used in place of nouns or adjectives and are divided into categories (personal, I or we; demonstrative, there or that; interrogative, where or whose; indefinite, one; distributive, each or either; reflexive, himself, themselves).

Verbs — words of action or state. Thus, to behave or to feel. Transitive verbs take an object, intransitive verbs do not. A transitive verb can be used in both the Active and the Passive, while an intransitive verb can only be used in the Active. For example: I clean the car (Active); The car was cleaned by me (Passive). The verb, to clean, is transitive. The sentence, I laugh loudly, however, uses the intransitive verb, to laugh. The word, loudly, is an adverb.

Adverbs — words which describe either verbs or adjectives. They usually have the suffix, -ly.

Prepositions — words which denote relationship between words or phrases. For example, to, for, under.

Conjunctions — these connect words, phrases, or sentences. And, but, although are good examples.

Interjections — words or phrases that stand outside the form of a sentence. They express emotion — Goodness me! Help! Hurrah! Oh!

Meanings and origins of some familiar words and phrases

There are many words and phrases commonly used today which go back hundreds of years. Here are some of the more familiar ones, with their meanings and probable origins:

A.1

Meaning: excellent, first-rate.

Origin: British ships are built to Lloyds Register of Shipping Regulations. One built to conform to the strictest Regulations is classed A.1. Hence, of the highest quality.

Baker's dozen

Meaning: 13 instead of 12.

Origin: from the habit of bakers at one time giving 13 rolls to the dozen to avoid being fined for selling underweight.

Bury the hatchet

Meaning: to make up a quarrel.

Origin: Red Indians, when they made peace with their enemies, would bury their weapons to show their good faith and to ensure that the war should not break out again.

Cock and bull story

Meaning: story which cannot be believed.

Origin: a Papal Bull is an edict made by the Pope and sealed with the Pope's seal, which bears a figure of St. Peter and a cock. After the Reformation, Papal Bulls went unheeded, and consequently any incredible tale is a 'cock and bull story'.

Cold shoulder

Meaning: to give someone the cold shoulder is to ignore him.

Origin: to discourage unwelcome visitors, a hostess merely served them with the remains of the joint, a fairly plain hint that they were not to call again.

Feather in one's cap

Meaning: something one may be proud of.

Origin: from the habit of Red Indians of sticking a feather in their head-dresses for every enemy they had slain.

Hobson's choice

Meaning: a choice that is really no choice at all, since the alternative would be nothing.

Origin: in the 17th century, Tobias Hobson kept a stable at Cambridge, from which he hired out horses. Although all his horses were ostensibly for hire, he would allow only the one nearest the door to be chosen, so that his horses were ridden in strict rotation. Any objection was met with the firm comment, 'It's that or none.'

Knuckle under, to

Meaning: to submit or to yield.

Origin: in Anglo-Saxon and Mediaeval English, the knuckle refers to the knee-joint as well as the finger-joints. To knuckle under, therefore, meant to bow the knee.

Mad as a hatter

Meaning: crazy

Origin: the phrase has nothing to do with hatters nor with madness. It was originally 'mad as an atter.' Atter was the Anglo-Saxon word for a viper or adder, and mad meant venomous. The expression thus meant as venomous as a viper.

On tenterhooks

Meaning: to be taut with anxiety.

Origin: after weaving, cloth is fixed by hooks to a frame and stretched so that it will dry evenly, without shrinking. The hooks are known as tenterhooks.

Post haste

Meaning: in a hurry.

Origin: in coaching days, a person wishing to get somewhere quickly would arrange for a relay of horses at the posting stations along his route.

Raining cats and dogs

Meaning: pouring with rain.

Origin: probably a corruption of an obsolete French word, *catadoupe,* which means a heavy fall of water.

Rule of thumb

Meaning: rule based on experience or practice.

Origin: it is said to have arisen from the habit of brewers in Yorkshire of dipping their thumbs into the vat to determine the heat of the liquor.

That's the ticket

Meaning: that's just right.

Origin: a corruption of the French *étiquette* meaning that is what you should do.

Uncle Sam

Meaning: the United States of America.

Origin: the story goes that a man named Elbert Anderson of New York had a store yard on the Hudson River. A Government inspector named Samuel Wilson, who was always known as Uncle Sam, used to examine the stores, marking the packages he had passed, EA-US, the initials of Elbert Anderson and the United States. One of the employees was asked what the initials stood for and replied facetiously that the US stood for Uncle Sam. The story spread and soon Uncle Sam became the nickname for America, just as John Bull for England.

White elephant

Meaning: something that is quite useless and often expensive to maintain.

Origin: in Siam, a white elephant was regarded as sacred. When the King of Siam wanted to be rid of the services of one of his courtiers, he would make him a present of a white elephant. The cost of keeping the animal usually ruined the poor man.

White feather, to show the

Meaning: to be a coward.

Origin: from cock-fighting days, when no true-bred gaming cocks ever had a white feather. If a cock had one, he was a crossbred and probably no great fighter.

Yankee

Meaning: an American.

Origin: from the first attempts by the North-American Indians to pronounce the word, English.

Abbreviations

A.A.	Automobile Association
A.A.A.	Amateur Athletic Association
a/c	account
A.T.C.	Air Training Corps
A.W.O.L.	absent without leave
B.A.	Bachelor of Arts
Bart.	Baronet
B.C.	before Christ, British Columbia
B.R.	British Rail
B.Sc.	Bachelor of Science
C.I.D.	Criminal Investigations Department

C.-in-C.	Commander-in-Chief
C.O.D.	cash on delivery
D.A.	District Attorney
F.A.	Football Association
F.B.I.	Federal Bureau of Investigation (US), Federation of British Industries
G.L.C.	Greater London Council
G.M.T.	Greenwich Mean Time
G.P.	General Practitioner
Hi-Fi	high frequency
H.Q.	headquarters
H.R.H.	His (or Her) Royal Highness
I.Q.	intelligence quotient
J.P.	Justice of the Peace
L	Latin, learner
L.T.A.	Lawn Tennis Association
M.C.	Master of Ceremonies
M.C.C.	Marylebone Cricket Club
M.D.	Doctor of Medicine
Messrs	plural of Mr
M.O.D.	Ministry of Defence
Ms	Mrs or Miss
N.A.A.F.I.	Navy, Army and Air Force Institutes
N.A.T.O.	North Atlantic Treaty Organisation
N.H.S.	National Health Service
O.H.M.S.	On Her (or His) Majesty's Service
P.A.Y.E.	Pay As You Earn
P.O.W.	Prisoner of War
P.R.O.	Public Relations Officer
R.A.C.	Royal Automobile Club
R.A.D.A.	Royal Academy of Dramatic Art
R.I.B.A.	Royal Institute of British Architects
R.N.L.I.	Royal National Lifeboat Institution
R.S.P.C.A.	Royal Society for the Prevention of Cruelty to Animals
R.S.V.P.	*répondez s'il vous plait* (please reply)
S.D.P.	Social Democrat Party
S.O.S.	distress signal, possible abbreviation of Save Our Souls!
S.R.N.	State Registered Nurse
T.N.T.	Trinitrotoluene (explosive)
T.T.	teetotaller, Tourist Trophy, tuberculin tested
T.U.C.	Trades Union Congress
U.N.	United Nations
U.N.E.S.C.O.	United Nations Educational, Scientific and Cultural Organisation
V.I.P.	very important person
W.I.	West Indies, Women's Institute
Y.H.A.	Youth Hostels Association
Y.M.C.A.	Young Men's Christian Association
Y.W.C.A.	Young Women's Christian Association

Words and Latin Phrases in Common Use

Ad hoc	for this purpose
ad infinitum	to infinity
ad nauseam	to a sickening degree
anno Domini	in the year of our Lord
ante	before
ante meridiem	before noon
bona fide	genuine
circa	about, around
de facto	in fact, really
et cetera	and so on
ex gratia	an act of grace
ex officio	by reason of office
ibidem (ibid.)	in the same book, chapter
id est (i.e.)	that is
idem	the same
in extremis	in extreme difficulties, at the point of death
in memoriam	in memory
in perpetuum	for ever
in situ	in its place
in toto	as a whole, in entirety
inter alia	among others
ipso facto	by the fact itself
magnum opus	great work, an author's main work
modus operandi	method of operation
modus vivendi	way of living
nil desperandum	don't despair
non compos mentis	of unsound mind
non sequitur	it does not follow
nota bene (NB)	note well
opere citato	in the work named
pari passu	with equal pace, together
per capita	per head
persona non grata	person who is unacceptable
post meridiem	afternoon
post mortem	after death
prima facie	at first sight
pro rata	in proportion
pro tempore	for the time being
quid pro quo	tit for tat
quod vide	which see (shortened to q.v.)
sic	thus, so
sine qua non	an indispensable condition
status quo	as things stand, the same state
stet	let it stand, ignore correction
tempus fugit	time flies
terra ferma	solid ground
verbatim	word for word
vide	see

The Arts

An Outline of European Architecture

Architecture is the art of building. Broadly speaking, buildings can be divided into three kinds: those having a religious purpose, such as temples and churches; civic buildings, such as houses, town halls and hospitals; and military, e.g. castles and fortifications. The history of European architecture is very briefly summed up in the following periods.

Classical

The architecture of ancient Greece — more specifically that of the period from the 7th century B.C. to the middle of the 4th century B.C. The Greek temple is often said to be the most perfect example of beauty in architecture. The best known building of the period is the Parthenon at Athens. Classicism in art and architecture in a wider sense has come to mean any style that has the qualities characteristic of the Greek styles, i.e. simplicity of form and restraint as opposed to exuberant styles.

Roman

Roman temples continued to follow the lines of those of the Greeks until the time of the Caesars. From the Etruscans (a people of Asiatic origins) the Romans learned the principle of the keystone which made possible the building of rounded arches and vaulted roofs. The typical Roman public building was known as a *basilica* which consisted of a large oblong hall flanked by columns with an aisle on each side. At the far end was a semi-circular area called an apse. This type of building was adapted by the early Christians for their churches. The Romans discovered the use of concrete which enabled them to build very large edifices such as their amphitheatres.

Byzantine

The architecture of the Christian Byzantine Empire which reached its peak in the 9th and 12th centuries A.D. The Byzantine church was based on the Roman basilica but was generally extended on a cruciform plan. Typically it was surmounted by a large dome placed on a square base consisting of four piers supporting four arches. The most perfect example of a Byzantine church is that of Hagia Sophia in Istanbul.

Romanesque

An early Mediaeval style of architecture prevalent in Europe between the period of Charlemagne (9th century) and the rise of the Gothic style. It was a fusion of different traditions and varied in different areas, but everywhere the round 'Roman' arch was used for windows, doors and arcades.

Gothic

A style prevalent in Northern Europe from the 13th to the 16th centuries. Gothic buildings have certain features in common: the pointed arch, the flying buttress and the rib-vault. The pointed arch made possible the building of very lofty churches and cathedrals, roofed with stone (vaults). The slender pillars of the nave supported the vaulting whose outward thrust was counterbalanced by flying buttresses. The structure allowed for plenty of windows; stained glass greatly added to the beauty of Gothic cathedrals.

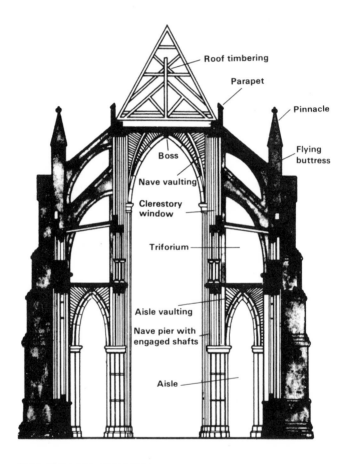

Some of the main style points
of Gothic construction are shown in this diagram

Renaissance

Meaning 'rebirth', the Renaissance was a movement originating in Northern Italy in the 14th century and which spread over western Europe in the 16th century. Hitherto the church had been the sole patron of the arts, but now patronage of a wealthy new merchant class enabled an artist or architect to express himself more freely.

Baroque

A style that developed in the 17th century, Baroque continued into the 18th century. Heavily ornate to the point sometimes of being grotesque, the style is noted for its sense of movement and excitement. The overall effect is one of magnificence and grandeur.

Rococo

An elegant, decorative style, characterised by delicate colours and asymmetrical patterns based on S and C shapes. This style began in France and was encouraged by King Louis XIV. It grew out of the Baroque and dated from about 1715 to the outbreak of the French Revolution in 1793.

20th Century

In the 19th century architectural styles had tended to look to the past for inspiration. Modern architecture has reached a complete independence of the past. New processes and new materials have given new possibilities of expression. However, economic considerations together with the mass production of parts has very often resulted in stark, square towers of glass, steel and reinforced concrete.

Movements in Modern Art

Realism

This movement began in the mid-19th century with Gustave Courbet. He reacted against the romantic, ideal art of the time and turned to the actuality of everday life for his subjects.

Impressionism

This was the most important art movement of the 19th century. It started in France in the 1860s. The name was derived from a picture by Monet, 'Impression, Sunrise' (1872). To create the illusion of light Monet and his followers broke up the colours of their pictures into small dabs of pure pigment. They tried to capture the play of light on the surface of objects and even shadows were rendered with colours. Leading exponents of Impressionism also include Seurat, Renoir and Pissarro.

Post Impressionism

Post Impressionism developed as a reaction against Impressionism, and returned to once more stressing the importance of the subject, the composition and the feeling of their pictures. Van Gogh, Gauguin and Cézanne can be considered as Post-Impressionist painters.

Expressionism

A style of art originating early in the 20th century, chiefly in Germany. Rather than the representation of nature it was concerned with personal emotion expressed through distortion, exaggeration and strong colour. The movement consisted of two groups. The first was called Die Brücke (The Bridge) because it formed a link between like-minded artists, and the second group was called Der Blaue Reiter (The Blue Rider). Expressionists include the artists Klee, Marc, Kandinsky and Kokoschka.

Fauvism

Fauvism means 'the wild beasts' and was a name derogatively applied to a group of artists whose works were exhibited together in Paris in 1905. These works were full of distorted forms and violent colours applied regardless of the actual colours of the subjects. Matisse is regarded as the leader of the Fauves; others were Derain, Vlaminck and Rouault. By 1908, however, the group had disbanded.

Cubism

This was developed by Pablo Picasso and Georges Braque. Influenced by African sculpture and also the paintings of Paul Cézanne, they experimented in ways of showing objects from several different viewpoints at the same time as a means of suggesting their shape and volume on a flat canvas. Using only drab tones at first, the Cubist painters introduced brighter colours after 1912 and began to add pieces of other materials to create what are known as *collages.* The first exhibition of Cubist pictures was in 1907.

Futurism

Futurism was an art and literary movement started by the Italian poet Filippo Tommaso Marinetti who glorified violence, war and the machine age — Futurists believed that their new art form expressed the age in which they lived. A notable characteristic of Futurist painting stemmed from the principle of 'simultaneity'. Figures and objects were represented in successive stages of motion superimposed on one another. The first Futurist paintings appeared in 1911 but the movement died out by 1915. Leading exponents were Severini, Boccioni, Balla and Garra.

Dadaism

The movement began in Zürich and was born out of the disillusion felt by many due to the First World War. Its aim was to outrage and scandalise, and overthrow all standards and traditions in art. Lasting only from 1915 to 1922, its foremost figures were Duchamp, Ernst, Picabia and Miro.

Surrealism

Dadaism developed into Surrealism and was founded by André Breton in 1924. Its object was to create out of the subconscious mind, reconstructing the world of dream and fantasy. In the work of the Spanish Surrealist painter Salvador Dali highly detailed representations of objects appear in strange, often distorted situations.

Great Historical Museums and Art Galleries

Name	Location	Name	Location
Acropolis Museum	Athens	Museum of Fine Arts	Boston
Alte Pinakothek	Munich	National Gallery	London
Bibliotèque Nationale	Paris	National Gallery of Art	Washington
British Museum	London	National Museum	Athens
Cairo Museum	Cairo, Egypt	National Museum	Naples
German Museum	W. Berlin	Prado	Madrid
Kunsthistoriches Museum	Vienna	Rijksmuseum	Amsterdam
Lateran Museum	Rome	State Museum	E. Berlin
Louvre	Paris	State Historical Museum	Moscow
Metropolitan Museum of Art	New York	Tate Gallery	London
Musée de Cluny	Paris	Uffizi Gallery	Florence
		Vatican Museum	Rome

Famous Music Festivals

Name and Place	Time of Year
Aix-en-Provence International Festival	July
Bayreuth, Richard Wagner Festival	July–August
Berlin (West), International Festival of Music and the Arts	September–October
Besançon International Festival of Music	September
Edinburgh International Festival	August–September
Glyndebourne Festival Opera, near Lewes, Sussex	May–August
Llangollen International Musical Eisteddfod	July
Munich Festival	June
Salzburg Festival	Easter and July–August
Wiesbaden International Festival	May
Würzburg Mozart Festival	June

Famous Films

The films listed overleaf generally represent the cream of their kind and are famous for any number of reasons: their magnificent acting, their powerful direction or simply, whatever one's own opinion of their merits, they made millions at the world's box-offices. An asterisk indicates that the film concerned won an Academy Award actually as a film (rather than for acting, direction, photography, screenplay, etc.).

Adventure
The Adventures of Robin Hood (1938), with Errol Flynn and Olivia De Havilland. *Beau Geste* (1940), with Gary Cooper and Susan Hayward. *Jaws* (1975), with Roy Scheider and Robert Shaw. *King Kong* (1933), with Fay Wray and Bruce Cabot. *La Grand Illusion* (1937), with Erich Von Stroheim and Pierre Fresnay. **Seven Samurai* (1954), with Toshiro Mifune.

Cartoons
Animal Farm (1952). *Bambi* (1941). *Fantasia* (1940). *Snow White and the Seven Dwarfs* (1937). All these were Walt Disney Productions, with the exception of Animal Farm, which was made in Britain by John Halas and Joy Batchelor.

Comedy
*Annie Hall (1977), with Woody Allen and Diane Keaton. *The General* (1928), with Buster Keaton. *The Gold Rush* (1925), with Charlie Chaplin and Mack Swain. *Kind Hearts and Coronets* (1948), with Dennis Price and Alec Guinness. *Monsieur Hulot's Holiday* (1951), with Jacques Tati. **The Music Box* (1932), with Stan Laurel and Oliver Hardy. *A Night at the Opera* (1935), with the Marx Brothers. **Tom Jones* (1963), with Albert Finney and Susannah York.

Drama
*Bicycle Thieves (1946), with Lamberto Maggiorani and Enzo Staiola. *Citizen Kane* (1941), with Orson Welles and Joseph Cotten. *The Graduate* (1969), with Dustin Hoffman and Anne Bancroft. **The Lost Weekend* (1945), with Ray Milland and Jane Wyman. **Ordinary People* (1980), with Donald Sutherland and Mary Tyler Moore. **Rebecca* (1940), with Joan Fontaine and Laurence Olivier. **Rocky* (1976), with Sylvester Stallone and Talia Shire.

Epics and Historical Drama
Battleship Potemkin (1925), directed by Sergei Eisenstein. **Ben-Hur* (1959), with Charlton Heston and Stephen Boyd. *Birth of a Nation* (1915), directed by D. W. Griffith. **The Deer Hunter* (1978), with Robert DeNiro and Meryl Streep. **Gone with the Wind* (1939), with Clark Gable and Vivien Leigh. **Laurence of Arabia* (1962), with Peter O'Toole and Alec Guinness. *The Virgin Spring* (1960), with Max Von Sydow and Birgitta Pettersson.

60

Horror

The Birds (1963), with Rod Taylor and Tippi Hedren. *Bride of Frankenstein* (1935), with Boris Karloff and Elsa Lanchester. *The Cabinet of Dr. Caligari* (1919), with Conrad Veidt and Lil Dagover. *Dracula* (1957), with Peter Cushing and Christopher Lee. *Invasion of the Body Snatchers* (1956), with Kevin McCarthy and Dana Wynter. *Onibaba* (The Hole) (1964), directed by Kaneto Shindo. *Vampyr* (1931). Directed by Carl Dreyer.

Musicals

Coal Miner's Daughter (1980), with Sissy Spacek and Tommy Lee Jones. *The King and I* (1956), with Deborah Kerr and Yul Brynner. *On the Town* (1949), with Gene Kelly and Vera-Ellen. *Singin' in the Rain* (1952), with Gene Kelly and Debbie Reynolds. *West Side Story* (1961), with Natalie Wood and Richard Beymer.

Science Fiction and Fantasy

La Belle et la Bête (1946), with Jean Marais and Josette Day. *Un Chien Andalu* (1928), directed by Luis Buñuel. *Close Encounters of the Third Kind* (1977), with Richard Dreyfuss. *Metropolis* (1926), with Brigitte Helm and Rudolph Klein-Rogge. *The Seventh Seal* (1957), with Gunnar Bjornstrand and Max Von Sydow. *Star Wars* (1977), with Mark Hamill and Harrison Ford. *Things to Come* (1936), with Ralph Richardson and Margaretta Scott. *2001: a Space Odyssey* (1967), with Keir Dullea and Gary Lockwood.

Thrillers

La Bête Humaine (1938), with Jean Gabin and Simone Simon. *The French Connection* (1971), with Gene Hackman and Roy Scheider. *The Godfather* (1971), with Marlon Brando and Al Pacino. *Little Caesar* (1931), with Edward G. Robinson and Douglas Fairbanks Jnr. *M* (1931), with Peter Lorre. *Public Enemy* (1930), with James Cagney and Jean Harlow. *The Third Man* (1949), with Joseph Cotten, Orson Welles and Valli.

Westerns

Butch Cassidy and the Sundance Kid (1969), with Paul Newman and Robert Redford. *Guns in the Afternoon* (1961), with Joel McCrea and Randolph Scott. *High Noon* (1952), with Gary Cooper and Grace Kelly. *The Magnificent Seven* (1961), with Yul Brynner and Steve McQueen. *Shane* (1953), with Alan Ladd and Jean Arthur. *Stagecoach* (1939), with John Wayne and Claire Trevor.

A Portrait of Henry Winstanley

Perhaps he was impetuous, perhaps even a little roguish, yet Henry Winstanley was certainly great. To him the impossible was always a challenge, a born showman's dream, a new world to conquer. His whole life forms an amusing, incredible story—the stuff of which folklore is made.

Born in 1664, a country lad from the sleepy market town of Saffron Walden in Essex, the young Henry started employment as 'my lord's porter' at the palace home of the Earl of Suffolk. Naturally inventive and skilled in drawing, he first gained attention by selling to the parish a clock so intricate that it was impossible to repair—a brilliant opening for a born practical joker. This, and other lively ventures, finally brought him to the notice of the 'Merry Monarch', King Charles II, after which a spectacular career was assured.

Swiftly gaining money and popularity, he made his own home at Littlebury a kind of funfair of mechanical pranks and bizarre contraptions, the startling house becoming known as 'Winstanley's Wonders'. Chairs would trap visitors or carry them across a pond into a tree; mirrors caused phantoms and amusing illusions. Since Henry thoughtfully fitted the house with a turnstile and charged admission, his finances increased with his fame. Soon made 'Clerk of Works' to the King, he worked more tableaux wonders, including trick effects with fire and water, in fashionable London.

Yet the shrewdly light-hearted and inventive Jester was destined to show a more serious side—an engineering feat even the government had not dared to take on. It was prompted by the terrible toll of ships and men taken by a triple reef, the dreaded red rocks of Eddystone, menacing the sea approach to Plymouth harbour. The very name Eddystone means 'the stone of the reeling waves', and all seamen of Europe feared it and added to its grim legends.

A lighthouse on these terrible rocks became vital, and Henry Winstanley volunteered to achieve the impossible, though even to inspect the rocks meant up to eight hours of hard and dangerous rowing. With an inspired team of the West Country's sturdiest men, he somehow managed to sink twelve iron uprights, sealed by molten lead, into the almost impenetrable granite. The conditions of working and the perils were appalling. Even worse was the actual construction work, prefabricated blocks of stone had to be carried out by boat and cemented in place for the solid base.

War with France and Henry's capture by a French sloop temporarily interrupted the work, but so impressed by him was King Louis XIV, that he was returned to England as a hero, loaded with rich gifts, and the work went on. As season followed season the incredible tower was somehow completed and, on November 14, 1698, Henry Winstanley mounted inner steps to the lantern and proudly lit the large tallow candles himself. Plymouth went wild! Visitors poured to the region and packed every vantage point; the shore festivities had to be experienced to be believed.

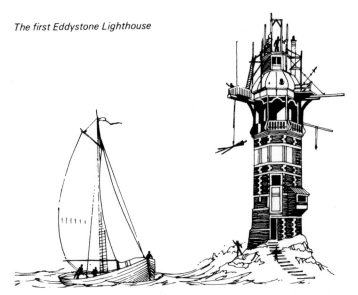

The first Eddystone Lighthouse

Not that Henry enjoyed them, for a storm stranded him and his team in their lighthouse for the following five weeks. The sea had struck back!

The miracle had been achieved but, except by grateful seamen, was very soon in danger of being forgotten and, as times changed, Henry's fame was beginning to suffer the same fate. That is, until the lighthouse's sixth winter, November 1703, when tower and base again needed urgent repair. Henry Winstanley and a small but intrepid team of labourers again set out . . .

It was bound to happen! That night came the storm—the *great storm*—the storm of all storms, the worst ever recorded in British history. Between midnight of November 26 and the following dawn, 8,000 sailors perished, church spires vanished, trees were uprooted in thousands—devastation scarred cities, towns and small villages.

Saturday's dawn saw no light gleaming from the red, sea-lashed rocks of the Eddystone. There was no lighthouse, no Henry Winstanley, no keeper, no labourers! Of the once proud tower all that remained were bent, twisted bars of metal protruding from rock like the stumps of rotted teeth in the red jaws of some primeval monster.

The curtain had come down with suitable flourish on a great showman who had once said he would like to be in his lighthouse 'during the greatest storm that ever was'. The desire had been granted, and it is quite possible that he would have approved. Everything about him had been larger than life, and the greatest storm seemed an appropriate climax. He had been an innovator, the first—yet now others would follow. An Eddystone Lighthouse would rise again and, despite other disasters, would always remain!

World-Famous People

Obviously it is possible to list only a small fraction of the world's many famous men and women—but here is a selection of those most outstanding in their fields of achievement.

Art, Sculpture, Architecture
Bernini, Giovanni Lorenzo (1598–1680), Italian sculptor, architect and painter in the Baroque style.
Botticelli, Sandro (1444–1510), Florentine Painter.
Le Corbusier (1887–1965), Swiss architect and town planner.
Dali, Salvador (1904–), Spanish surrealist painter.
Leonardo da Vinci (1452–1519), Italian painter, sculptor and architect.
Michelangelo (1475–1564), Italian painter, sculptor and architect.
Monet, Claude (1840-1926), French painter; the leading impressionist.
Picasso, Pablo (1881-1973), Spanish painter. One of the founders of the Cubist movement.
Raphael (1483-1520), Italian painter of the Renaissance period.
Rembrandt, Harmensz van Rijn (1606-69), Dutch painter.
Rodin, Auguste (1840-1917), French sculptor.
Titian (c. 1487–1576) the greatest Venetian painter.
Turner, Joseph Mallord William (1775–1851). English landscape painter.
Van Gogh, Vincent (1853–90), Dutch Post-Impressionist painter.
Velazquez, Diego (1599–1660), regarded by many as Spain's most notable painter.
Wren, Christopher (1632–1723), English architect whose greatest achievement was St. Paul's Cathedral in London.

Exploration
Amundsen, Roald (1872–1928), Norwegian. The first to reach the south pole and to navigate the north-west passage.
Armstrong, Neil (1930–), American astronaut. The first man to set foot on the Moon. With him was Edwin Aldrin.
Columbus, Christopher (1451–1506), Italian explorer of the New World.
Cook, James (1728–79), English sea captain who made voyages to New Zealand and Australia. He was murdered by natives at Hawaii attempting to find the north-west passage.
Diaz, Bartolomeu (fl.1481 – 1500), Portuguese explorer who discovered the Cape of Good Hope
Eric the Red (10th c.), Viking explorer who discovered Greenland.
Gama, Vasco da (c. 1469–1524), Portuguese navigator, the first man to travel from Europe to India by sea.
Magellan, Ferdinand (c. 1480-1521), Portuguese explorer. He commanded the first expedition to sail round the world.
Polo, Marco (1254–1324), Venetian explorer of China.
Tasman, Abel (1603-59), Dutch navigator who discovered Tasmania and New Zealand.

Literature

Balzac, Honoré de (1799–1850), French novelist.

Burns, Robert (1759–96), National poet of Scotland.

Byron, Lord (1788–1824), English poet.

Cervantes, Miguel (1747–1816), Spanish creator of DON QUIXOTE.

Chekhov, Anton (1860–1904), Russian dramatist.

Dante (1265–1321), Italian poet, author of the DIVINE COMEDY.

Dickens, Charles (1812–70), English novelist.

Dostoyevsky, Fyodor Mikhailovich (1821–81), Russian novelist.

Euripides (480–406 B.C.), Greek tragic dramatist.

Goethe, Johann Wolfgang von (1749–1832), Germany's greatest poet.

Homer (c. 8th–7th c. B.C.), author of epic poems, the ILIAD and the ODYSSEY.

Hugo, Victor (1802–85), French novelist, poet and playwright.

Ibsen, Henrik (1828–1906), Norwegian dramatist.

Khayyám, Omar (11th c.), Persian poet.

Milton, John (1608–74), English Puritan, poet and prose writer.

Molière (1622–73), dramatist. Greatest writer of French comedy.

Pushkin, Alexander (1788–1837), Russia's greatest poet and dramatist.

Schiller, Johann Friedrich von (1759–1805), German dramatist and poet.

Scott, Sir Walter (1771–1832), Scottish romantic novelist and poet.

Shakespeare, William (1564–1616), greatest English dramatist, and a poet.

Sophocles (c. 496–406 B.C.), Greek dramatist.

Tolstoy, Count Leo (1828–1910), Russian novelist.

Voltaire (1694–1778), French essayist, playwright and novelist who attacked the injustices of his time.

Virgil (70–19 B.C.), Roman poet.

Music and Dance

Bach, Johann Sebastian (1685–1750), German composer.

Beethoven, Ludwig von (1770–1827), German composer.

Caruso, Enrico (1873–1921), Italian tenor—perhaps the greatest singer of the 20th century.

Chopin, Frédéric (1810–49), composer of music for the piano. Born near Warsaw, Poland.

Diaghileff, Serge (1872–1929), director of Russian ballet.

Fonteyn, Dame Margot (1919–), English prima ballerina.

Grieg, Edvard (1843–1907), Norwegian composer.

Liszt, Franz (1811–86) Hungarian composer and perhaps the world's greatest ever pianist.

Melba, Dame Nellie (1861–1931), Australian soprano.

Mozart, Wolfgang Amadeus (1756–91), Austrian composer.

Nijinsky, Vaslav (1890–1950), Russian ballet dancer and choreographer.

Schubert, Franz Peter (1797–1828), Austrian composer.

Schumann, Robert (1810–56), German composer.

Stradivari, Antonio (1644–1730), Italian, the greatest of all violin-makers.

Stravinsky, Igor (1882–1971), Russian composer.

Tchaikovsky, Peter Ilyich (1840–93), Russian composer.

Wagner, Richard (1813–83), German composer of operas.

Invention

Baird, John Logie (1888-1946), Scottish television pioneer.

Bell, Alexander Graham (1847-1922), inventor of the telephone. Born in Scotland, he went to America in 1870.

Benz, Karl (1844-1929), German engineer whose motor car (1885) was one of the first to be driven by an internal combustion engine.

Bessemer, Sir Henry (1813-98), English inventor of the process for converting cast-iron into steel.

Cockerell, Christopher (1910-) English inventor of the hovercraft.

Diesel, Rudolf (1858-1913), German engineer who invented an internal combustion engine.

Edison, Thomas Alva (1847-1931), American inventor of, among other things, the gramophone and incandescent light.

Harrison, John (1693-1776), English inventor of the chronometer.

Marconi, Guglielmo (1874-1937), Italian pioneer of wireless telegraphy.

Watt, James (1736-1819), Scottish inventor of the steam piston engine (1765), an improvement on earlier steam engines pioneered by Thomas Savery (1698) and Thomas Newcomen (1712).

Whittle, Sir Frank (1907-), English pioneer of jet propulsion.

Wright, Orville (1871-1948) and *Wilbur* (1867-1912), the American builders of the first aeroplane.

Science and Mathematics

Copernicus, Nicolas (1473-1543), Polish astronomer who maintained that the planets and the earth revolve round the sun.

Curie, Marie (1867-1934), born in Poland, and her husband *Pierre Curie* (1859-1906), a Frenchman, joint discoverers of radium.

Darwin, Charles (1809-82), English naturalist famous for his theory of Evolution.

Einstein, Albert (1879-1955), mathematical physicist, famous for his Theory of Relativity. Born in Germany but worked also in Switzerland and the U.S.A.

Fleming, Sir Alexander (1881-1955), Scottish bacteriologist who discovered Penicillin.

Galileo (1564-1642), Italian. His experimental methods laid the foundations of modern science.

Kepler, Johann (1571-1630), German scientist who discovered the laws of planetary motion.

Leibnitz, Gottfried Wilhelm (1646-1716), German mathematician who invented the calculus (1684).

Lister, Joseph (1827-1912), English surgeon who established the need for antiseptic methods in surgical operations.

Mendel, Gregor (1822-84), Bohemian monk who discovered the laws of biological inheritance.

Newton, Sir Isaac (1642-1727), English mathematician and scientist famous for his theory of gravitation. He invented the calculus independently of Leibnitz but his work was not published until 1687.

Pasteur, Louis (1822-95), French chemist who founded the sciences of bacteriology and immunology.

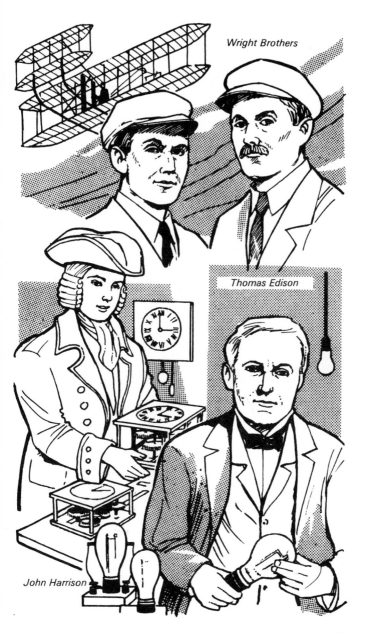

Wright Brothers

Thomas Edison

John Harrison

World Calendars

The Roman Calendar

The Romans used a calendar that dated from the Foundation of Rome (753 B.C. according to our own calendar reckoning). Their year was 304 days long, divided into ten months, beginning with March. Later, the months of January and February were added, making a total of 355 days in the year. About 700 years after the Foundation of Rome, Julius Caesar discovered that the Calendar had fallen into confusion . With the help of an Egyptian astronomer, he redesigned the calendar so that the year became 365 days long, with an extra day every fourth year (the Leap Year). The Julian Calendar, as it came to be known, is the one on which our own calendar is based.

The Gregorian Calendar

Sometime around the sixth century A.D., the numbering of the years was changed to start with the Birth of Christ and each year was signified by the letters A.D. or *Anno Domini* (in the year of Our Lord). The letters B.C. (Before Christ) denote the years before the birth of Jesus and are counted backwards. Thus, 300 B.C. is *earlier* than 200 B.C., while 300 A.D. is *later* than 200 A.D. In other respects, the Christian Calendar was the same as the Julian Calendar. However, in 1582, it was found that making *every* fourth year a Leap Year had resulted in a discrepancy of about ten days. Pope Gregory decided to lose the extra ten days and ordained that October 5, 1582, should be called October 15, and that in future only one in four of the end-of-century years should be Leap Years. In this way, neither 1800 nor 1900 were Leap Years but the year 2000 will be. The Gregorian Calendar was gradually adopted by the countries of the world over the next 400 years. The change-over was made in England in 1752, when Wednesday, September 2, 1752, was followed by Thursday, September 14.

The Jewish Calendar

The starting point of the Jewish Calendar corresponds to October 7, 3761 B.C. It is based on the Jewish belief that the Era of Creation occurred at the time of the Autumnal Equinox in 3760 B.C. The normal calendar year of the Jews is divided into 12 months and lasts only 354 days, but so that there shall not be too great a difference from the solar year, a thirteenth month is occasionally added to the Jewish year.

The Moslem Calendar

The Moslem Calendar starts with the *Hejira*, or the flight of Muhammad from Mecca to Medina, which corresponds to July 16, A.D. 622

The Ancient Greek Calendar

The Ancient Greeks reckoned their time in *Olympiads*, which were cycles of four years corresponding to the Olympic Games held on the plain of

Olympia every fourth year. Each Olympiad was given the name of the victor at games. The first Olympiad we know about is that of Choroebus, 776 B.C.

Leap Years
The length of a year corresponds to a solar year, or the time the Earth takes to go round the Sun. However, the average solar year is 365.242 days and the seasons would eventually be thrown into confusion if the extra quarter of a day were not taken into account. To maintain a proper balance, therefore, every fourth year contains one extra day, making 366 in all. The extra day is February 29. It occurs in those years that are divisible by four: for example, 1972, 1976, 1980, etc. But there is yet one more complication concerned with Leap Years. The solar year is in fact not quite 365 ¼ days long and this means making another small adjustment. Consequently, centennial years (1300, 1700, 1900, etc) are treated as ordinary years unless the first two figures of the year are divisible by four. 1200 and 1600 were leap years, 2000 will be one too, because 12, 16 and 20 are all divisible by four.

The Seasons
In the Northern Hemisphere, the four seasons are:
Spring from the Vernal Equinox (about March 21) to the Summer Solstice (June 21).
Summer from the Summer Solstice to the Autumnal Equinox (about September 21).
Autumn from the Autumnal Equinox to the Winter Solstice (about December 21).
Winter from the Winter Solstice to the Vernal Equinox. In the Southern Hemisphere, the seasons are reversed, Spring corresponding to Autumn, Summer to Winter, Autumn to Spring and Winter to Summer. We think of Christmas Day as falling in mid-Winter and are delighted if snow falls and we get a White Christmas. But if you lived in Australia, you would celebrate Christmas in the Summertime and eat your turkey in the sunshine.

The Solstices are the days of the year when the Sun is furthest from the Equator. The Summer Solstice, therefore, in the Northern Hemisphere is the longest day (in terms of daylight), the Winter Solstice the shortest day.

The Equinoxes occur when the Sun crosses the Equator and day and night are of equal length.

Easter Day. Unlike Christmas Day, which is always December 25, Easter Day is a movable feast. According to English Law, it is calculated as the first Sunday following the first full moon after the Vernal (or Spring) Equinox. Many people would like Easter to become a fixed feast, and in 1928, Parliament passed the Easter Act, which would have fixed Easter Days as 'the first Sunday after the second Saturday in April'. However, the Act required the support of the various international Churches and this was not given. So, for the time-being at any rate, Easter remains a movable feast.

The Months of the Year

Name	Named after	Length in days
January	Janus, Roman god of the portal, who faces two ways, the past and future.	31
February	Februa, Roman Festival of Purification.	28 (29 in Leap Year)
March	Mars, Roman god of war (originally the 1st month).	31
April	Aperire, Latin verb 'to open'. When the earth opens to receive seed.	30
May	Maia, Roman goddess of growth and increase.	31
June	Junius, from the Latin gens, meaning family.	30
July	Julius Caesar. At one time, the month was called Quintilis or 5th month.	31
August	Julius Caesar Augustus. Formerly Sextilis or 6th month.	31
September	Septem, meaning seven, or 7th month.	30
October	Octo, eight, 8th month.	31
November	Novem, nine, or 9th month.	30
December	Decem, ten, or 10th month.	31

The Days of the Week

Name	Named after
Monday	Moon's Day
Tuesday	Tiu's Day. Tiu is the Anglo-Saxon counterpart of Tyr, the Nordic god of war, and son of Odin.
Wednesday	Woden, Anglo-Saxon for Odin, Nordic messenger of victory.
Thursday	Thor, Nordic god of thunder, eldest son of Odin.
Friday	Frigg's Day. Frigg or Freyja was the wife of Odin and Nordic goddess of love.
Saturday	Saturn's Day
Sunday	Sun's Day

Greenwich Mean Time

Time in the British Isles is known as *Greenwich Mean Time*. During the summer months, however, *British Summer Time* operates, when the clocks are one hour ahead of G.M.T. This gives us one hour's extra daylight in the evenings, reducing by one hour the amount of daylight before we get up in the morning. B.S.T. is in force usually from March to October and throughout this period our time is the same as the Continent's. From 1968 to 1971, *British Standard Time* operated, which meant that our clocks were one hour ahead of G.M.T. throughout the year. Public outcry, however, forced the Government to return to G.M.T. in October, 1971.

Standard Time

In 1883, *International Time Zones* were established. The world is now divided into 24 time zones or segments, each measuring 15° of longitude. The 12 zones to the west of Britain are behind Greenwich Mean Time, while the 12 zones to the east are in front of G.M.T. To avoid confusion, however, most countries have established a standard time which applies throughout the country. The standard time is loosely based on the international time zones. Some countries which are very large (like the United States) have more than one standard time. The table below shows the time in some of the major cities of the world when it is 1200 hours G.M.T., or 1300 hours B.S.T. in London.

Adelaide, Australia	2130 hours
Aden	1500 hours
Algiers, Algeria	1400 hours
Amsterdam, Holland	1300 hours
Antwerp, Belgium	1300 hours
Athens, Greece	1400 hours
Auckland, New Zealand	2400 hours
Baltimore, U.S.A.	0700 hours
Berlin	1300 hours
Bermuda	0900 hours
Bombay, India	1730 hours
Borneo	2000 hours
Boston, U.S.A.	0700 hours
Brisbane, Australia	2200 hours
Buenos Aires, Argentina	0900 hours
Cairo, Egypt	1400 hours
Calcutta, India	1730 hours
Cape Town, South Africa	1400 hours
Chicago, U.S.A.	0600 hours
Copenhagen, Denmark	1300 hours
Hong Kong	2000 hours
Honolulu	0200 hours
Leningrad, U.S.S.R.	1500 hours
Lima, Peru	0700 hours
Mecca	1440 hours
Melbourne, Australia	2200 hours
Mexico City, Mexico	0500 hours
Montreal, Canada	0700 hours
New Orleans, U.S.A.	0600 hours
New York, U.S.A.	0700 hours
Odessa, U.S.S.R.	1500 hours
Perth, Western Australia	2000 hours
Paris, France	1300 hours

Rangoon, Burma	1830 hours
San Francisco, U.S.A.	0400 hours
Singapore	1930 hours
Stockholm, Sweden	1300 hours
Sydney, Australia	2200 hours
Tokyo, Japan	2100 hours
Vancouver, Canada	0400 hours
Wellington, New Zealand	2400 hours
Winnipeg, Canada	0600 hours

The International Date Line, or line where the change of date occurs, runs down the 180th meridian, or 180° longitude, with a few variations for geographical or political reasons.

Watches at Sea

The 24 hours of the day are divided at sea into watches, each four hours long except for the period between 1600 hours and 2000 hours which is split into two two-hour dog watches. The watches are known as follows:

2400-0400 hours	Middle Watch
0400-0800 hours	Morning Watch
0800-1200 hours	Forenoon Watch
1200-1600 hours	Afternoon Watch
1600-1800 hours	First Dog Watch
1800-2000 hours	Second Dog Watch
2000-2400 hours	First Watch

Useful Tables

Angles

60 seconds (")	= 1 minute (')
60 minutes	= 1 degree (°)
90 degrees	= right angle or quadrant
4 right angles	= 1 circle (360°)

Time

60 seconds	= 1 minute
60 minutes	= 1 hour
24 hours	= 1 day
7 days	= 1 week
52 weeks and 1 day	= 1 year
365 days	= 1 year

Weight (Troy—used for measuring gold and silver)

24 grains	= 1 pennyweight
20 pennyweights	= 1 ounce Troy

Metric Weights and Measures

Length

10 millimetres	= 1 centimetre
10 centimetres	= 1 decimetre
10 decimetres	= 1 metre = 100 centimetres
10 metres	= 1 dekametre
10 dekametres	= 1 hectometre
10 hectometre	= 1 kilometre = 1,000 metres

Area

100 square metres	= 1 are
10 ares	= 1 dekare
10 dekares	= 1 hectare
100 hectares	= 1 square kilometre

Weight

10 milligrams	= 1 centigram
10 centigrams	= 1 decigram
10 decigrams	= 1 gramme
10 grammes	= 1 dekagram
10 dekagrams	= 1 hectogram
10 hectograms	= 1 kilogram = 1,000 grammes
10 kilograms	= 1 myriagram
10 myriagrams	= 1 quintal
10 quintals	= 1 tonne = 1,000 kilograms

Capacity

10 millilitres	= 1 centilitre
10 centilitres	= 1 decilitre
10 decilitres	= 1 litre
10 litres	= 1 dekalitre
10 dekalitres	= 1 hectolitre

Mathematics: Symbols

·	decimal point	<	less than
+	plus	>	greater than
−	minus	≥	equal to or greater than
±	plus or minus	≤	equal to or less than
×	multiplied by	≃	approximately equal to
÷	divided by		
=	equals	≯	not greater than
≠	does not equal	≮	not less than
≡	congruent to	√	square root
△	triangle	r^n	r to the power of n
%	per cent	‖	parallel to
‰	per thousand	∦	not parallel to

Mathematical Formulae

Triangle
Area = ½ base × height

Square
Area = side × side

Circle
($\pi = 3\cdot14159$)
Diameter (d) = 2 × radius (r) = 2r
Circumference = $2\pi r$ or πd

Area = πr^2 or $\dfrac{\pi d^2}{4}$

Quadrant = 90°. 4 quadrants = 360° = circle

Sphere
Volume = $\dfrac{4\pi r^3}{3}$ 　　　　　 Surface area = $4\pi r^2$

Cone
Volume = $\dfrac{\pi r^2 h}{3}$

Curved surface area = πr × slant height (l) or πrl

Cylinder
Curved surface area = $2\pi rh$ 　 Volume = $\pi r^2 h$
Total surface area = $2\pi rh + 2\pi r^2 = 2\pi r(h + r)$

74

Ellipse
(major axis = 2a, minor axis = 2b)   Area = πab

Pyramid
$$\text{Volume} = \frac{\text{Area of the base} \times \text{perpendicular height}}{3}$$

Trapezium
$$\text{Area} = h \times \frac{(\text{parallel sides added together})}{2}$$

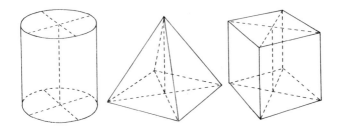

Cylinder   *Pyramid*   *Trapezium*

The Greek Alphabet

The word 'alphabet' is derived from the first two letters of the Greek alphabet. It is included in the mathematical section because so many of its letters are used as mathematical symbols. Pi (π) is a good example.

Alpha	A	α	Nu	N	ν
Beta	B	β	Xi	Ξ	ξ
Gamma	Γ	γ	Omicron	O	o
Delta	Δ	δ	Pi	Π	π
Epsilon	E	ϵ	Rho	P	ϱ
Zeta	Z	ζ	Sigma	Σ	σ, s
Eta	H	η	Tau	T	τ
Theta	Θ	θ	Upsilon	Υ	υ
Iota	I	ι	Phi	Φ	ϕ
Kappa	K	$\varkappa$	Chi	X	χ
Lambda	Λ	λ	Psi	Ψ	ψ
Mu	M	μ	Omega	Ω	ω

Roman Numerals

Rules

When a letter is repeated, the value of the number is increased by the value of that letter. E.g. XX = 20, CCC = 300, MMM = 3,000.

Letters are placed in order of value, the letter of smaller value increasing the amount of the whole number by the amount of the smaller. E.g. VII = 7, LXII = 62.

A letter placed before another letter of greater value decreases the number by the value of the smaller letter. E.g., IX = 9, XL = 40, CM = 900, MCM = 1,900.

A bar placed over a letter or group of letters multiplies the value by 1,000 E.g. $\overline{X}$ = 10,000, $\overline{XL}$ = 40,000.

I—	1	XX—	20	MCC—	1,200
II—	2	XXX—	30	MCCC—	1,300
III—	3	XL—	40	MCD—	1,400
IV or IIII—	4	L—	50	MD—	1,500
V—	5	LX—	60	MDC—	1,600
VI—	6	LXX—	70	MDCC—	1,700
VII—	7	LXXX—	80	MDCCC—	1,800
VIII—	8	XC—	90	MCM—	1,900
IX—	9	C—	100	MM—	2,000
X—	10	CC—	200	MMM—	3,000
XI—	11	CCC—	300	$\overline{IV}$—	4,000
XII—	12	CD or CCCC—	400	$\overline{V}$—	5,000
XIII—	13	D—	500	$\overline{X}$—	10,000
XIV—	14	DC—	600	$\overline{L}$—	50,000
XV—	15	DCC—	700	$\overline{C}$—	100,000
XVI—	16	DCCC—	800	$\overline{D}$—	500,000
XVII—	17	CM—	900	$\overline{M}$—	1,000,000
XVIII—	18	M—	1,000		
XIX—	19	MC—	1,100		

Mach Numbers

If you have heard or read any reports on supersonic aircraft, you may have noticed the term Mach (pronounced Mark) when reference is made to the aircraft's speed. A Mach Number is the ratio of an object's speed to the local speed of sound in similar surrounding conditions. Mach 1.0 at sea-level at standard pressure and temperature is the equivalent of 1,225 km. per hour. In the stratosphere, however, the equivalent to Mach 1.0 is some 163 km./h slower at 1,062 km./h. The term Mach is named after Ernst Mach, a professor of physics at Prague, Czechoslovakia, who died in 1916. Stratospheric Mach Numbers in terms of km./h are shown in the table below:

Mach 1.0	1,061.78 km./h	Mach 5.0	5,308.92 km./h
Mach 2.0	2,123.57 km./h	Mach 6.0	6,370.70 km./h
Mach 3.0	3,185.35 km./h	Mach 7.0	7,432.49 km./h
Mach 4.0	4,247.13 km./h		

Cookery

Cooking is easy, providing you keep it simple. Learn to know your tools before you start cooking and then follow a few simple rules. Your most important tool is the cooker, which is usually either gas or electric. In gas ovens the heat is cool at the bottom, hotter in the middle and very hot at the top. Any setting given in a recipe is for the *middle* of the oven. The change of temperature is not so marked in an electric cooker.

The hob is the top of the cooker, on which pans are placed for boiling, steaming, or frying. Most cookers have a grill, which is used to direct fierce heat onto one side of the food being cooked. The food is then turned to cook on the other side. Grilling is best used for tender meat and some types of fish.

Equipment
A few utensils are needed: bowls or basins for mixing, pots and pans for cooking plus a few cooking tools, such as a sharp knife, fork, spoons. Keep your equipment as basic as possible and wash up as you go along, so that you do not end up with a kitchen full of dirty dishes and spoons.

Basic ingredients needed in cooking are as follows:
Dairy Products, used in cakes, pastry, for omelettes etc. Butter, eggs, cheese.
Groceries, for general cooking. Bacon, ham, cooked meats, margarine, lard, cooking fats, olive or corn oil, vinegars.
Flour, for pastry, cakes, biscuits, etc.
Sugar, for sweetening.
Spices, Salt, Pepper used to add flavour.

Cooking Vegetables
Green Vegetables: Broccoli, Cabbage, Brussels Sprouts, Cauliflower, Peas, Spinach.

Bring a minimum amount of salted water to the boil and place vegetables in pan. Bring to the boil and then turn down heat to simmer veg. for about four minutes. Remove from heat and drain through a colander. Toss in butter before serving. Spinach should be cooked for about three minutes in only a few drops of salted water. *Never* overcook vegetables.
Root Vegetables: Carrots, Parsnips, Potatoes, Swedes, Turnips

Remove outer skin of vegetables with a knife or peeler. Wash thoroughly and place in a bowl of water until ready to cook. Place in pan of boiling salted water and simmer for approximately ten minutes. Test with a fork for softness which indicates that vegetables are cooked.

Potatoes can be cooked in many ways; here are two methods which you may prefer to boiling:
Baked Potatoes: Choose large potatoes, scrub skin clean with a brush and prick with a fork. Brush with oil and place in the oven in the hottest part. Cook for one hour. Serve with butter.

Mashed Potatoes: Boil potatoes until soft and drain off water. Break up the potatoes with a fork or vegetable masher in the pan. Add a large knob of butter or margarine and a small measure of milk if desired. Whisk together until the potato is soft and fluffy.

Soft Vegetables: Tomatoes and Mushrooms

These can be grilled or fried. Always use fresh mushrooms and wipe them clean with a damp cloth. Cut off the end of the stalks and peel back the skin off the tops. Cook by grilling for about a minute or by dropping into hot fat for two minutes. (Take great care to avoid splashes of hot fat.) Tomatoes should be wiped clean, cut in half and cooked as for the mushrooms.

Salads: Lettuce, Tomatoes, Radishes, Beetroot, Cucumber

These should always be washed well and eaten raw. You can combine all the above ingredients and for variety add fruits. Try adding stawberries or peaches to lettuce, or apples dipped in lemon juice to retain their colour.

Always make sure that the lettuce is fresh and only prepare it just before eating, otherwise it will wilt. Take off damaged outer leaves, cut away stem and wash in slightly salted water. Toss dry, making sure that all surplus water is removed.

Cooking with Eggs

Boiled eggs: There are two methods: either place the eggs carefully in boiling water then turn down to simmer until the egg is cooked, or place the eggs in cold water, bring to the boil and then reduce the heat to simmer. How hard or how soft the eggs are depends on personal taste. 10 to 12 minutes will cook a hard-boiled egg, and 5½ to 7 minutes a soft-yolked egg and 3 to 4 minutes a soft-boiled egg. Time from the moment you turn the heat down.

Coddled eggs: For a perfectly soft cooked egg. Place eggs in pan of boiling water. Remove at once from heat and cover with a lid. Leave large eggs for 9 minutes and small eggs for 6 minutes.

Scrambled eggs: Place small amount of fat in pan and allow to melt over a low heat. Crack required amount of eggs into bowl and whisk with a fork. For every two eggs add a small quantity of milk. Season with salt and pepper and pour into pan. Stir with a fork or spoon until egg is cooked.

Omelettes: Use two or three fresh eggs and crack into a bowl. Whisk with a fork adding salt and pepper to taste. Heat a small amount of butter into frying pan so that thin layer of fat covers base. Add egg mixture and increase the heat. Cook quickly for about 80 to 90 seconds, slip onto a warm plate and serve immediately. For variety, try filling omelettes with ham, cheese or mushrooms.

Cookery Terms

Bouquet garni	Small muslin bags filled with herbs used for flavouring stews, casseroles, etc.
Croquettes	Cone-shaped balls of minced meat, fish or potatoes, egg-and-breadcrumbed and fried
Croûtons	Fried or toasted bread, cut in pieces and served in soup

Escalope	Thin slice of meat, usually veal
Flan	Open tart, cooked in a ring
Frappé	Iced
Hors-d'Oeuvre	Dish of tasty morsels served at the beginning of a meal
Marinade	Liquid containing herbs and seasoning in which meat, fish or vegetables are soaked before cooking
Mornay	With a cheese sauce
Navarin	A stew of lamb or mutton
Paté	Savoury mixture of finely minced liver
Purée	Pulp of vegetables or fruit put through a sieve
Roux	A mixture of melted fat and flour which forms the basis for many sauces
Sauté	Fried in shallow fat
Vinaigrette	Mixture of oil, vinegar and seasonings
Vol-au-vent	Case of puff pastry

British Measures

⅛ pint = ½ gill = 4 tablespoons = ¼ cup British Standard Measure = 71 ml.
¼ pint = 1 gill = 8 tablespoons = ½ cup British Standard Measure = 142 ml.
1 pint = 2 cups British Standard Measure = 0.568 litre
1 quart = 2 pints = 4 cups British Standard Measure = 1.14 litres
1 gallon = 4 quarts = 8 pints = 16 cups British Standard Measure = 4.5 litres

American Measures

1 American pint = 16 fluid oz. = 0.454 litre
1 British pint = 20 fluid oz. = 0.568 litre
1 American cup measure = 8 fluid oz. = 227 ml.
1 American tablespoon = 3 flat teaspoons
(All American spoon measures are a flat spoonful)
1 American cup of flour = 4½ oz. = 127 g.
1 American cup of sugar = 7 oz. = 198 g.
1 American cup of butter = 7 oz. = 198 g.
1 American tablespoon of flour = ½ oz. = 14 g.
1 American tablespoon of sugar = ¾ oz. = 21 g.
1 American tablespoon of butter = ¾ oz. = 21 g.

Oven Temperatures

	Temperature	Regulo	Main Setting
Very slow	240°–280°F	¼–½	A–B
Slow	280°–320°F	1	C
Warm	320°–340°F	3	C
Moderate	340°–370°F	4	D
Fairly hot	370°–400°F	5–6	E
Hot	400°–440°F	7	F
Very hot	440°–480°F	8–9	G–H

Health and Nutrition

Nutrition and a Balanced Diet

Your body needs food for three reasons:

1. It supplies fuel that keeps you warm and gives you energy.
2. It provides the raw materials needed for growth.
3. It supplies the vitamins, proteins and minerals that are essential to the body's chemical processes.

When your energy reserves need restocking, your stomach passes on the message by means of hunger pangs. It also tells you when to stop eating by that 'full-up' feeling. If you take no notice of this warning and carry on eating then the surplus food is not converted into energy but into extra weight.

Energy-Providing Foods

The principal fuels, or energy-providing foods, are *carbohydrates* (found in sugar and starchy foods, such as bread, cereals and potatoes), and *fats* (found in fatty meat and dairy products). The materials essential to the growth and repair of body tissues are *proteins* (richest sources meat, fish, cheese, nuts and wheat germ). *Vitamins* and *minerals* supply the protective element: vitamins help to keep the various organs and tissues healthy, while minerals (such as iron, calcium, phosphorus and iodine) provide minute but vital components of blood, bones and teeth.

While everything you eat contains some of these essential elements, it is important that the right amount be taken. This is achieved through following a well-balanced diet.

Quantity is important to healthy living and remember that the amount of food we need is not just decided by our size and weight. You may be smaller than your father and yet need at least as much fuel as he does, mainly because you are still growing and he is not.

Calorie Intake

A Calorie is used to calculate the amount of energy produced in the human body by different kinds of food.

Everything we do demands some kind of energy output, though obviously some activities use up more Calories than others. Running uphill would certainly burn them up fast, but a lively game of football is just as effective and much more fun!

When you are young and still growing your daily fuel requirement is probably between 2,500 and 1,900 Calories. The exact amount depends of course on your age, your build and how active you are. Some of the Calories will come from the protein foods, but most from carbohydrates and fats.

Roughage

Fresh fruit and leafy green vegetables are not only rich in vitamins and minerals, they are also our main source of roughage. Roughage (coarse-

Calorie and Nutrition Chart

Food	Average portion	Calories	Protein	Fat	Carbo-hydrate	A	B group	C	Minerals
						Rich or fairly rich source of Vitamin			
Bacon (fried)	2 rashers	310	√	√			√√		√√
Beef (roast)	75 gm	260	√	√			√		√
Blackcurrants	100 gm	60						√	√
Bread (wholemeal)	1 slice	65			√		√		
Butter	25 gm	200		√		√			
Cabbage	125 gm	20						√	
Carrots	100 gm	20				√√			
Cheese (Cheddar-type)	25 gm	110	√	√		√	√	√	√√
Chicken (roast)	100 gm	225	√				√		
Chocolate (milk)	50 gm	280		√	√		√√		
Cod/haddock (grilled)	100 gm	160	√				√		
Eggs (boiled)	1	90	√√						
Ham	50 gm	230	√√	√			√√		√
Honey/jams/marmalade	50 gm	160			√				
Liver (ox)	50 gm	120	√			√	√√√	√	√√
Milk	175 ml (1 cup)	120	√	√			√√√		
Oranges	1	70						√	
Peanuts	50 gm	340	√	√					
Potatoes (boiled or baked)	100 gm	115			√				
Rice (boiled)	175 gm	600			√				
Sardines (tinned)	75 gm	180	√				√		√√
Sausages (large pork)	2	380		√		√			√√
Spinach	37 gm	20						√	√√
Wheat germ	50 gm	240	√		√		√		√√√

fibred, bulky foods which take longer to pass through the digestive system), has only recently come to be fully appreciated. Modern refining and preserving processes have removed a lot of roughage from our diet with the result that diseases of the digestive system are now more common than they once were. Other sources of roughage are bran (the nutritious husk of grain — tasty of fruit and cereal), dates, raisins, figs, prunes and whole grain cereals.

Vitamins

A well-balanced diet — one that includes meat, fish, dairy products, fresh fruit and vegetables — normally contains all the vitamins essential for good health. These are the vitamins most important to good health:

Vitamin A plays a role in how the eye perceives light; lack of this vitamin can lead to poor vision in dim light. It also helps to prevent dryness of the skin and internal membranes, and so protects against infection.

The richest source of Vitamin A is oil from the liver of such fish as cod and halibut. An indirect but important source is a substance called *carotene*, which the body can convert into Vitamin A. Foods rich in carotene include carrots, egg yolks, butter, yellow or orange fruits and the outer, dark-green leaves of vegetables.

Vitamin B is in fact a group of vitamins, usually referred to by their chemical names (for examples, thiamine, riboflavine, nicotinic acid and folic acid) but known as the *Vitamin B complex.* Not a great deal is known about their functions, but B-complex vitamins are known to play a part in the reactions that convert food into energy. They also help in the formation of blood cells.

The most abundant sources are liver and yeast; but B vitamins are found also in eggs, milk, wheat germ, pork and leafy vegetables.

Look at the chart on the previous page to see the Calorie and nutrition value of some common foods.

Vitamin C (ascorbic acid) is essential to tissue growth, to healthy gums and mouth, and to natural healing of cuts and broken bones. Richest sources are citrus fruits (lemons, oranges, grapefruit) and all green vegetables, especially watercress and cabbage.

However, Vitamin C is lost very quickly if food is overcooked or stored.

Vitamin D plays a part in the formation of bones and teeth. It is found in milk, butter, margarine, cheese, eggs and fish-liver oils, and is produced in skin exposed to sunlight.

The functions of *vitamin E,* present in most foods but especially abundant in vegetable oils are still not clear; while *vitamin K,* found in leafy green vegetables, is known to have a roll in the blood-clotting process.

Watching Your Weight

The 'Ideal Weight' for your height is calculated by statistics; and statistics, being both complicated and impersonal, can never give more than a very general, overall picture. Very few young people are truly overweight or underweight, it depends very much on your build. Heredity (the pattern of physical characteristics you inherit from your parents), is the major factor in how quickly and how much you grow.

If you make a point of including in your diet plenty of fresh fruit and greens, and remember to go easy on high-carbohydrate foods, you should stay healthy and at the right weight.

Exercise

When our apelike ancestors first began to stand on their hind legs, it was a great step forward: from that day on they were free to use their hands creatively. But this posture also brought problems. The human skeleton was designed for a creature that moved most efficiently on all fours; and the spine in particular did not easily adapt to the upright position.

Since we are still suffering to some degree from this evolutionary defect, it is important that we stand properly to try to avoid backaches.

To stand properly, hold your head well up (but relaxed, not stiff), your chest high, your bottom flat and your back slightly hollowed. Always sit well back in your seat, rather than slumped forward or sideways. When walking, hold your body firm so that your legs do most of the work. Crouch rather than bend when you lift a heavy object from ground level, so that again the legs take the strain.

All sports help with muscle development, but walking and cycling are also excellent means of exercise, because they use every muscle in the body and improve the efficiency of heart, lungs and circulation.

Dental Care

Dental caries (the medical name for tooth decay) is the most widespread of all human diseases. The worst culprits in tooth decay are such foods as sweets, biscuits, puddings and cakes, jams and sweetened drinks, all of which cling to the teeth and thus encourage the formation of *plaque* (bacteria-ridden deposits of food debris which cause decay and sometimes gum disease).

The best protection against the build-up of plaque is regular brushing. Brush after every meal if possible (downwards for upper teeth and gums, upwards for lower teeth and gums). Remember that the acid produced in plaque begins to eat into your tooth enamel within 15 minutes of eating, so if you cannot clean your teeth after a meal then try to finish it off with a crisp apple. Finally, make sure you have regular check-ups to ensure that any little problem is dealt with early.

Drugs, Alcohol and Tobacco

Drugs

Drugs of many kinds have been of great benefit to mankind, especially over the last 50 years. Smallpox, tuberculosis, polio and many other once widespread diseases would still be killing millions annually but for the discovery of certain drugs. Tragically, however, there have also been disasters; babies born severely deformed as a result of their mothers' having taken the apparently safe drug thalidomide; small children accidentally poisoned by 'sweeties' that turn out to have been tablets prescribed for an adult; and people who have become addicted to drugs.

It is not advisable to experiment with any kind of drugs. The consequences can be very serious both medically and psychologically. It is also illegal, of course, to possess drugs such as cannabis, marijuana of LSD, and drugs such as heroin or cocaine without a doctor's prescription.

Alcohol
While the law forbids anyone under the age of eighteen to buy alcohol, it is not illegal to drink alcohol before that age. Alcohol is absorbed into the bloodstream and then depresses the function of all living cells. This means that it slows you down both mentally and physically; and when it is taken to excess it is literally poisonous to the system.

Cigarettes
Unlike the occasional drink, the occasional cigarette may be very harmful indeed—if only because almost everyone who starts by smoking 'just the odd one now and then', eventually finds himself or herself smoking regularly and heavily.

Most people find it hard to give up smoking. It was once believed that it was just a matter of willpower, but recent research suggests that the body does in fact become physically addicted to at least one of the substances contained in cigarettes. Quite apart from the important health aspects, it is a very expensive habit, and one that often repels non-smokers. It pollutes the atmosphere and endangers the health of others beside the smoker himself; asthma sufferers are particularly vulnerable to cigarette smoke. It is far better, therefore, to resist any temptation to try smoking cigarettes and steadfastly remain a non-smoker.

Your Changing Body
From the moment you are born your body is changing all the time. Every day worn-out cells are discarded and replaced by new ones. Awake or asleep, the busy body machine is always working, renewing, repairing, growing. We can feel some systems, like circulation, breathing and digestion. Other parts we can't see, *glands* regulate the body's functions by producing substances called *hormones*. Some glands have been at work since you were born; others start at different stages of growth, like clocks switching things on at set times. Some time after the tenth year the *gonads*, or sex glands, begin secreting special hormones. The exact age—any year between 11 and 15—depends on your own 'time clock'. Girls have female gonads: *ovaries*. Male gonads are the *testes*. These need to be cool to work properly, so they are not inside the body like the ovaries, but below it in a pouch of skin, the *scrotum.*

The Changes You Can See
As sex hormones begin circulating, they influence the way you grow and you change by degrees. The baby fuzz on arms and legs is replaced by hair. Now thicker growths, *pubic* hair around your penis and scrotum and under your arms, are usually the first signs of hormone activity. Male pubic hair grows in a diamond shape up towards the navel. Much later the beard begins to show, starting on your upper lip. Some men grow hair on the chest and back. The skin is also developing *sweat* and *sebaceous* glands which make *sebum,* a grease to protect and lubricate the skin.

Gradually over two or three years, the testes get larger and your penis grows. You take on a masculine shape as you grow in height and your shoulders become broader.

Finally your voice changes. It doesn't really 'break'. Your voice box, the *larynx,* grows and you acquire deeper chest tones—hard to control until you are used to them. Don't worry if some boys seem ahead of you. You will catch up in your own time. Growth is very individual and changes can occur in any order; they are entirely controlled by your personal body chemistry.

Hygiene

All body secretions, if not cleaned off, smell strong and unpleasant. Sweat and grease glands, especially in the armpits, the groin and the feet, are working extra hard. Personal hygiene is especially important, so take extra care to clean these places thoroughly.

Skin on your face and back also needs extra care to avoid spots. Bath brushes and loofahs help to reach your shoulders and back. Above all, wash your hands and brush your nails as often as you can. If your hands aren't clean, *keep them off your face.* Dirty hands cause boils, pimples and other skin troubles.

Sebum from the oil glands on your face and back is often overproduced, so most people have acne (spots) at some stage. Sebum blocks the pores, the blockage attracts dirt, and you have a 'blackhead'. If the blocked glands get infected, pimples or lumps can occur. Avoid greasy foods and chocolate. Careful washing, using coaltar soap with a very soft brush, is the best answer. There are good specific creams and your doctor can help if it is really bad.

Coming to Terms with Your New Self

As you grow taller, you'll find that people expect you to behave as an adult. You may well feel very uncertain and strange, so here are some of the problems and a few ideas for coping with them.

Those busy hormone-making glands get out of balance at times. They make you confused and moody. You feel angry or frustrated for no real reason, or you get low, depressed and believe no one loves you. Your family won't always know how you feel or how to treat your changing moods. Rows and quarrels flare up quickly. But while a row can clear the air and release tension don't let quarrelling become a habit. Other people can't be wrong *all* the time.

Of course *you* are the most interesting person in your life now. However you aren't so important to everyone else. They can see you as self-centred, stroppy, even selfish, if you hog the bath, play your choice of music long and extra loud or use their things without asking. That sort of thing makes enemies. Imagine how other people feel; look at yourself with their eyes. Your behaviour affects everyone: other boys, teachers, parents and strangers. Just how likeable are you?

We can all be turned on by the way someone sings or performs. But some adolescents get obsessed by their idol—pop star, footballer or teacher—and they act, dress and talk like a bad imitation. Often it's

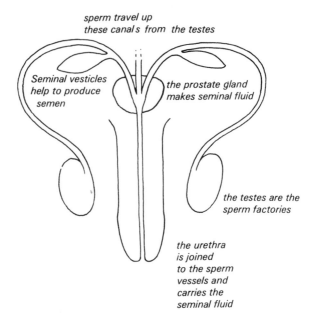

sperm travel up
these canals from the testes

Seminal vesticles
help to produce
semen

the prostate gland
makes seminal fluid

the testes are the
sperm factories

the urethra
is joined
to the sperm
vessels and
carries the
seminal fluid

because they don't want to face the hassle of growing up as themselves. Admiration is natural; being stuck like glue on someone is stupid. Copying won't make you Elton John; anything you want to achieve has to be done by the real *you*.

All this fast growing can make you feel lackadaisical and tired. You don't want to do anything but lie about and daydream. This often makes adults wild. They seem not to understand how slowly time goes by when the future is light-years away, and you won't know what it's like till you get there. It is easier to dream about it. In daydreams, of course, we are all wonderful, the greatest. But dreams are more fun if they have a chance of coming true. The hero of *your* dreams should be the person you really are. No point in being John Travolta if you have two left feet.

Parents dream too, and this can cause trouble. They'd like you to be a real world-beater. You must not only be honest with yourself about your abilities; you will have to convince them. It's natural that they want the best for you, but don't let their worries get on top of you. It's *your* life.

Remember, every adult was once an adolescent. They all had just the same problems and, as you see — *they survived.*

European Christian Names, their Origins and Meanings

Boys' Names
F = French   G = German   I = Italian   S = Spanish

Adam Adam (F)(G), Adamo (I), Adán (S). 'Red'. Hebrew.

Alexander Alexandre (F), Alex (G), Alessandro (I), Alejandro (S). 'Defender of Men'. Greek.

Andrew André (F), Andreas (G), Andrea (I), Andrés (S). 'Manly'. Greek.

Anthony Antoine (F), Anton (G), Antonio (I)(S). 'Inestimable'. Latin.

Arnold Arnaud (F), Arnold (G), Arnoldo (I), Arnaldo (S). 'Eagle'. Teutonic.

Augustus Auguste (F), August (G), Augusto (I)(S). 'Venerable'. Latin.

Bernard Bernard (F), Berhard (G), Bernardo (I)(S). 'Brave as a Bear'. Teutonic, Old English.

Charles Charles (F), Carl, Karl (G), Carlo (I), Carlos (S). 'Noble Spirit'. Teutonic, Old English.

Christopher Christophe (F), Christoph (G), Cristoforo (I), Cristobal (S). 'Bearer of Christ'. Greek.

Claud Claude (F), Claudius (G), Claudio (I)(S). 'Lame'. Latin.

Daniel Daniel (F)(G)(S), Daniele (I). 'God has Judged'. Hebrew.

David David (F)(G)(S), Davide (I). 'Beloved'. Hebrew.

Eric Erico (F)(I)(S), Erich (G).'Ever King'. Norse.

Ernest Ernest (F), Ernst (G), Ernesto (I)(S). 'Earnestness'. Teutonic.

Francis François (F), Franz (G), Francesco (I), Francisco (S). 'Frenchman'. Latin.

Frederick Frédéric (F), Friedrich, Fritz (G), Federico (I)(S). 'Peaceful Ruler'. Teutonic.

George Georges (F), Georg (G), Giorgio (I), Jorge (S). 'Farmer'. Greek.

Godfrey Godefroi (F), Gottfried (G), Goffredo (I), Godofredo (S). 'God's Peace'. Teutonic.

Gregory Grégori (F), Gregor (G), Gregorio (I)(S). 'Watchman'. Greek.

Harold Harold (F), Harald (G), Araldo (I), Haraldo (S). 'Great General'. Norse.

Henry Henri (F), Heinrich (G), Enrico (I), Enrique (S). 'Home Ruler'. Latin.

Hugh Hughes (F), Hugo (G)(I)(S). 'Heart, Spirit'. Teutonic.'

James Jacques (F), Jakob (G), Giacomo (I), Jaime, Diego (S). 'Supplanter'. Hebrew.

John Jean (F), Johann (G), Giovanni (I), Juan (S). 'Grace of the Lord'. Hebrew.

Joseph Joseph (F), Josef (G), Giuseppe (I), José (S). 'He shall increase'. Hebrew.

Lawrence Laurent (F), Lorenz (G), Lorenzo (I)(S). 'Laurel'. Latin.

Lewis, Louis Louis (F), Ludwig (G), Luigi (I), Luis (S). 'Famous Warrior'. Teutonic.

Luke Luc (F), Lukas (G), Luca (I), Lucas (S). 'Light'. Greek.

Mark Marc (F), Markus (G), Marco (I), Marcos (S). 'Mars (the War god)'. Latin.

Matthew Mathias (F), Matthias (G), Matteo (I), Mateo (S). 'Gift of God'. Hebrew.

Maurice Maurice (F), Moritz (G), Maurizio (I), Mauricio (S). 'A Moor'. Latin.

Michael Michel (F), Michel (I), Miguel (S), Michel, Michael (G). 'Like the Lord'. Hebrew.

Nicholas Nicolas (F), Nikolas (G), Nicolo, Nicola (I), Nicolás (S). 'Victory of the People'. Greek.

Paul Paul (F)(G), Paolo (I), Pablo (S). 'Small'. Latin.

Peter Pierre (F), Peter (G), Pietro (I), Pedro (S). 'Rock'. Greek.

Philip Philippe (F), Philipp (G), Filippo (I), Felipe (S). 'Lover of Horses'. Greek.

Ralph Raoul (F), Rudolf (G), Rodolfo (I)(S). 'Wolf'. Norse.

Raymond Rémond (F), Raimund (G), Raimondo (I), Ramón, Raimundo (S). 'Wise Protection'. Old French.

Reginald Renaud (F), Reinhold, Reinald (G), Rinaldo, Reinaldo (I), Reinaldo (S). 'Judgement'. Teutonic.

Richard Richard (F)(G), Riccardo (I), Ricardo (S). 'Ruler'. Old English.

Robert Robert (F)(G), Roberto (I)(S). 'Bright Fame'. Teutonic.

Roger Roger (F), Rüdiger (G), Ruggiero (I), Rogerio (S). 'Spear of Fame'. Teutonic.

Stephen Étienne (F), Stephan (G), Stefano (I), Esteban (S). 'Crown'. Greek.

Thomas Thomas (F)(G), Tomáso (I), Tomás (S). 'Twin'. Aramaic.

Victor Victor (F)(S), Viktor (G), Vittore (I).

Walter Gauthier (F), Walter (G), Gualtiero (I), Gualterio (S). 'Folk Ruler'. Teutonic.

William Guillaume (F), Wilhelm (G), Gugliemo (I), Guillermo (S). 'Helmet of Will'. Teutonic.

Girls' Names

Agatha Agathe (F)(G), Agata (I), Ágata, Águeda (S). 'Good'. Greek.

Agnes Agnès (F), Agnes (G), Agnese (I), Inés (S). 'Pure'. Greek.

Alice Alice (F)(G), Alicia (I)(S). 'Nobility'. Teutonic.

Amelia Amélie (F), Amalie (G), Amelia (I)(S). 'Vigour'. Teutonic.

Ann, Anne Anne (F), Anna (G)(I), Ana (S). 'Grace'. Hebrew.

Barbara Barbe (F), Barbara (G)(I)(S). 'Strange, Foreign'. Greek.

Beatrice Béatrice, Béatrix (F), Beatrix (G), Beatrice (I), Beatriz (S). 'Bringer of Happiness'. Latin.

Bertha Berthe (F), Berta (G)(I)(S). 'Bright One'. Teutonic.

Blanche Blanche (F), Blanka (G), Bianca (I), Blanca (S). 'White'. French.

Bridget Brigitte (F)(G), Brigida (I)(S). 'Strength'. Celtic.

Caroline Caroline (F)(G), Carolina (I)(S). A feminine form of Charles, 'Noble Spirit'. Old English, Teutonic.

Catherine Catherine (F), Katharine, Katrina (G), Caterina (I), Catalina (S). 'Pure'. Greek.

Charlotte Charlotte (F)(G), Carlotta (I), Carlota (S). A feminine form of Charles. 'Noble Spirit'. French.

Clare Claire (F), Klara (G), Chiara (I), Clara (S). 'Clear' or 'Famous'. Latin.

Constance Constance (F), Constanze, Constantia (G), Constanza (I), Constenza (S). 'Firm, Constant'. Latin.

Dorothy Dorothée (F), Dorothea (G), Dorotea (I)(S). 'Gift of God'. Greek.

Elizabeth Élisabeth (F), Elisabeth (G), Elisabetta (I), Isabel (S). 'Consecrated to God'. Hebrew.

Eva Eve (F), Eva (G)(I)(S). 'Life'. Hebrew.

Gertrude Gertrude (F)(I), Gertrud (G), Gertrudis (S). 'Spear Maiden'. Teutonic.

Helen Hélène (F), Helene (G), Elena (I)(S). 'The Bright One'. Greek.

Ida Ide, Ida (F), Ida (G)(I)(S). 'Hard Work'. Teutonic.

Irene Irène (F), Irene (G)(I)(S). 'Peace'. Greek.

Joan, Jane, Janet, Jean Jeanne (F), Johanna (G), Giovanna (I), Juana (S). Feminine form of John, 'Grace of God'. Hebrew.

Louise Louise (F), Luise (G), Luigia, Luisa (I), Luisa (S). Feminine form of Louis, 'Famous Warrior'. French.

Lucy Lucie (F)(G), Lucia (I)(S). 'Light'. Latin.

Madeleine Madeleine (F), Magdalene (G), Maddalena (I), Madelena (S). 'Woman of Magdala'. Hebrew.

Margaret Marguerite (F), Margarete (G), Margherita (I), Margarita (S). 'A Pearl'. Latin.

Martha Martha (F), Martha, Marthe, (G), Marta (I)(S). 'Lady'. Aramaic.

Mary Marie (F)(G), Maria (I)(S). 'Bitterness'. Hebrew.

Matilda Mathilde (F)(G), Matilde (I)(S). 'Mighty Battle-maid'. Teutonic.

Rachel Rachel (F), Rahel (G), Rachele (I), Raquel, Rachel (S). 'A Ewe'. Hebrew.

Rebecca Rébecca (F), Rebekka (G), Rebeca (S). 'A Snare'. Hebrew.

Sarah Sara (F)(G)(I)(S). 'Princess'. Hebrew.

Sophia Sophie (F), Sophia (G), Sofia (I)(S). 'Wisdom'. Greek.

Susan Suzanne (F), Susanne (G), Susanna (I), Susana (S). 'Lily'. Hebrew.

Therese Thérèse (F), Therese (G), Teresa (I)(S). 'Reaper'. Greek.

Pop and Rock Music

For centuries there have been popular forms of music, from songs of the travelling troubadour in the Middle Ages, through to the theatrical musical entertainment of the Victorian Music Hall. The invention of the gramophone and radio, however, have enabled the sound of a popular song to be reproduced on hundreds of thousands of records. Another important factor was the emergence of rock and roll—or rock 'n' roll, as it is better known—in the early 1950's in the United States. This style of music sparked off the many strands of music that are now classed as pop and rock.

Along with this came a new emphasis on groups, rather than individual singers, though the early rock 'n' rollers did tend to be soloists, like Elvis Presley, Carl Perkins, Ricky Nelson, Roy Orbison and Buddy Holly. They would use musicians who worked regularly in a particular recording studio to 'back' them when they recorded a song.

Elvis Presley

Elvis Presley began his phenomenal career by making a birthday record for his mother in the local Memphis Recording Service studio. He paid four dollars to make the record and the owner of the studio, Sam Phillips, suspected that Presley had potential and got two local musicians to provide backing. The record they made *That's All Right Mama,* was a local success, and so began Presley's rise to fame.

His early music is a perfect example of the beginnings of rock 'n' roll. It combined the Country Music that was the modern folk music of the American southern states white population, with black Rhythm and Blues. Presley's first few records, for instance, featured a blues song on one side and a country song on the other.

Rock 'n' Roll

In America in the 1940s *Rhythm and Blues* was the music of the 'ghettos'; those areas of the cities where the black population lived. It was made by black artists and sold through small record labels to the black population. To the rest of America (the white majority), it was known as 'race music'. Popular artists included singer/pianists such as Ray Charles, guitarists like B. B. King and Bo Diddley and old Bluesmen such as Howlin' Wolf.

The term 'rock 'n' roll' was first used in 1952 by radio disc jockey Alan Freed as a way of describing rhythm and blues without associating it with the black minority. This enabled him to popularise it with white audiences on his radio shows. This opened the doors for a new stream of white imitators, the first of which was Bill Haley, famous for *Rock Around The Clock*. Presley, Gene Vincent, Conway Twitty, Jerry Lee Lewis and many others were hugely successful with a new form of music that had some of the excitement of the raw, original black R & B but was acceptable to a big white record-buying public.

British Beat

Rock 'n' roll spread to Britain via Bill Haley's film of *Rock Around The Clock*. The film was enormously popular with teenagers, but the reaction it provoked was very worrying to some authorities. There was a warning of the hysterical reactions of teenage fans, when cinemas were wrecked by screaming Haley fans, and BBC radio would not play rock 'n' roll records.

The absence of the original American rock 'n' roll stars and their records, which were brought over by sailors and other visitors, left the way clear for impersonators such as Terry Dene, who made a successful version of Elvis Presley's *All Shook Up*.

Meanwhile British R & B had a healthy life in clubs, with artists like Georgie Fame, Zoot Money, John Mayall and the early Rolling Stones. Nevertheless, this was a small scale thing that grew out of the jazz scene. It took the beginnings of British Beat and the phenomenal success of one particular group to produce a genuinely popular British offshoot of rock 'n' roll. That group was The Beatles.

The Beatles

The Beatles are still the most important group in the rock and pop world. John Lennon, Paul McCartney, George Harrison and Ringo Starr were brought up in Liverpool, which was a port with strong American connections. There they were exposed to a lot of American rock 'n' roll records and they created their own, tough cheeky interpretation with their first record *Love Me Do* in December 1962, and with their next three, all of which became number ones: *Please Please Me, From Me to You* and *She Loves You*.

The Beatles were extremely successful in America too, starting a fashion for British groups in the U.S. charts. By continually absorbing new influences and always making their records sound very contemporary they stayed at the top until the end of the Sixties, when they split up and went their separate ways.

The Beatles

The Sixties

Despite the Beatles' success in America, most British popular music was influenced by American music. What the Beatles had achieved in the early sixties, however, was the transformation of R & B imitations into 'real' pop music. They used more complex, but still attractive, tunes and decorated them with lots of vocal harmonies and varied instruments.

As the decade went on, their music progressed even further, mixing classical and older popular music, folk, R & B into their greatest achievement, the *Sergeant Pepper's Lonely Hearts Club Band* LP. This established them as something even newer—the first rock band. This music was more ambitious, it was not contented with making simple three minute long tunes that would sound good on the radio and sell hundreds of thousands of copies. Rock wanted to be taken seriously.

Further influences came from America with singers such as Bob Dylan. He was a poet and folk singer, and he and the Beatles became the two biggest names in modern music. Dylan brought electric instruments and techniques of modern recording to his 'serious' folk background. It was very effective and in 1965 his song *Like a Rolling Stone* became number two in America.

The folk influence of the Sixties rock from groups like The Byrds, Grateful Dead and the Beach Boys, led to the softer sounds of the end of the decade and the so-called 'hippie' period. 'Love and Peace' became the catchphrase and in Britain 'psychedelic' groups like the Pink Floyd took up the theme.

The Seventies

Groups like the immensely popular Pink Floyd showed how completely pop had been abandoned in favour of rock in the early Seventies. They hardly played any songs, but performed long pieces of music with rambling structures making up each instrument's contribution as they went along. They took their music very seriously and spent more and more money on equipment, special lighting on stage and extravagant extras such as choirs and orchestras.

Most rock in the Seventies went this way—loud, grandiose and pompous. Two names stand out from this mass: Roxy Music and David Bowie. Both rose to fame in the early part of the decade in the time of 'glitter' or 'glam-rock', when the emphasis was on very theatrical and visually striking stage presentation. Both were very stylish and made very good records, with the toughness of rock but keeping the simplicity of pop. Both are still making records and are still very successful in the Eighties.

Punk and After

Punk was a violent reaction against the boring and pretentious rock of the mid-Seventies. It was crude, loud and nasty; many of the groups were proud of the fact that they couldn't play! The most popular punk was called, appropriately, Johnny Rotten. Punk didn't last long. It was more a fashion than a musical style.

After punk though, the importance of fashion in pop and rock was very much stronger. There have since been several revivals of previous musical fads such as Mod, Sixties R & B and Psychedelia. Groups like Madness or Ultravox create very popular styles of clothes and hair through having hit records. Now, in the early Eighties, some of the fun and energy of early pop has reappeared. Now rock and pop overlap more than ever; who knows what will happen next?

The Zodiac

The Zodiac is an imaginary belt in the heavens in which the paths of the sun, moon and major planets are supposed to lie. This is divided into 12 equal parts, each with its own Sign. Astrologers believe that the position of the sun, moon and planets within these Signs at the time of a person's birth has an effect on that person's character and destiny.

The Signs are:

Aries	The Ram	March 21 to April 19
Taurus	The Bull	April 20 to May 20
Gemini	The Twins	May 21 to June 21
Cancer	The Crab	June 22 to July 22
Leo	The Lion	July 23 to August 22
Virgo	The Virgin	August 23 to September 22

Libra	The Scales	September 23 to October 23
Scorpio	The Scorpion	October 24 to November 21
Sagittarius	The Archer	November 22 to December 21
Capricorn	The Goat	December 22 to January 19
Aquarius	The Water-carrier	January 20 to February 18
Pisces	The Fish	February 19 to March 20

Signs of the Zodiac

Aries

Libra

Taurus

Scorpio

Gemini

Sagittarius

Cancer

Capricorn

Leo

Aquarius

Virgo

Pisces

Nature Studies

Nature is everywhere and can be studied wherever you are — in the town, the country or by the sea. Studying nature can also be one of the cheapest pastimes. You do not have to have expensive binoculars, cameras, etc. The most important thing is being able to *observe*. For this you need a pair of sharp eyes and a good deal of patience. You will need to be able to identify the plants, birds or wild animals that you find, so you will have to refer to books from time to time to check their names. Taking notes and keeping good records is a very useful way of learning from your observations.

How to Tell the Difference
Insects and spiders
Insects have six legs and three body divisions: head, thorax and abdomen. They have antennae, which are sense organs.
Spiders have four pairs of legs and two body divisions. Instead of antennae they have little feelers called palps.

Spiders and harvestmen
Harvestmen are easily confused with *spiders*, having four pairs of slender legs and a pair of palps, but they are only distant relations. The harvestman's body is not divided into two parts and it spins no silk. It has two small pincers whereas the spider has fangs.

Butterflies and moths
All *butterflies* have antennae ending in a club or knob. *Moths* have many types of antennae but they are always without a knob, apart from the Burnet moths whose antennae have a rather similar thickening. The majority of moths have a special mechanism for coupling the wings together. This is a stout bristle projecting from the hind wing to the front wing, held in place by a little hook. Butterflies never have this device. It is a mistake to think that all moths fly by night — many fly during the daytime.

Bees, wasps and hoverflies
The *hoverflies* vary considerably in shape and colour. Some of them have mimicked the coloration of bees and wasps as a protection against predators. They hover over flowers and feed on nectar. You can readily tell the difference. *Bees* and *wasps* have two pairs of wings. Hoverflies, like all fly species, have only one pair of wings. The hoverfly wing characteristically has a vein running closely parallel with the wing edge. Notice, too, the large pair of compound eyes. A characteristic of bees, wasps and ants (all members of the same family) is a very narrow waist.

Common frog and common toad
The background colouring of the *common frog* is variable, ranging from yellowy brown to dark brown and tends to change with its surroundings.

There is always a dark band behind the eye and crossbars of the same colour on the legs. The *common toad* can tolerate drier conditions than the frog, and its limbs are shorter in proportion to the body. Its skin is earth-brown and warty-looking. Frog spawn is laid in jelly-like masses while that of the toad consists of double strings of similar-looking eggs. The frog tadpole tends to be lighter coloured and speckly; the toad tadpole is altogether duller.

Snake and slow-worm
A *slow-worm* looks very much like a snake but it is really a limbless lizard. The male can grow to about 45 cm. long and the female even longer. Its body is covered with tightly fitting, brownish, glossy scales which make the slow-worm look very smooth. You can identify the slow-worm by its eyes which are lidded and will blink. The *snake* can only stare.

Adder and grass-snake
A female *grass-snake* may measure 90 cm. or even longer; the male is rather shorter. The skin is light brown or greyish in colour with little black markings along the sides. There is also a yellow band behind the head which gives the snake the less common name of ringed snake. This snake is harmless but may surprise you by squirting an evil-smelling yellow fluid from its vent if it is handled. The poisonous *adder* (or viper) is variable in ground colour but is generally brownish, red-brown or greyish. Its most distinctive feature is the dark zig-zag marking running along its back from neck to tail and generally a clear V-sign on the head. A male adder can measure about 60 cm. The adder is common in dry heathlands and may be seen basking in the sun.

Rook and carrion crow
The *rook* is distinguished by its baggy thigh feathers and the bare greyish patch at the base of its bill. Rooks feed in groups and roost in colonies. *Crows* are seen together only in small family groups.

Swallow, house martin and swift
The *swallow* has a deeply forked tail and dark throat. The tail of the house martin is less forked. Its underparts are white as is its rump. The less common *sand martin* is identified by its brown back and a band across its chest. The *swift* looks very similar to martins and swallows but is not in fact related to them. Dark brown all over, it is rather larger than they are. Characteristically it screeches as it flies.

Rabbits and hares
Rabbits are smaller than hares. Their hind legs and ears are shorter in proportion. They sleep and breed in underground burrows. *Hares* have dark tips to their ears and long front legs. They sleep and breed in thick grass or vegetation.

Red deer, fallow deer and roe deer
The *red deer* is identified by its large size. A stag measures some 105 cm. at

the shoulder, the hind about 90 cm. The large branch-like antlers of the stag is another distinguishing feature. The *fallow deer* is only a little smaller than the red deer but it may be identified by its antlers which are flattened like the palm of the hand with little finger-like projections at the extremities. The coat is generally spotted with white. The *roe deer* is considerably smaller than the red and fallow deer, standing about 60 cm. at the shoulder. Its antlers are simpler and shorter and it has a white patch around its tail which shows up well in winter.

Field mushrooms and poisonous Amanita species
One of the most poisonous fungi is all-white and might be mistaken for an edible mushroom. The field mushrooms that you can eat all have grey or pink to chocolate brown coloured gills and no bag at the base of the stipe (stem).

Animal Tracks
The sketches below show some of the most familiar animal tracks. Look for them in dust, soft soil, mud or snow.

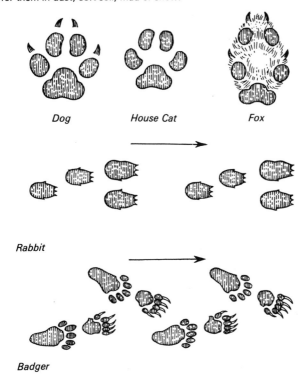

Dog   House Cat   Fox

Rabbit

Badger

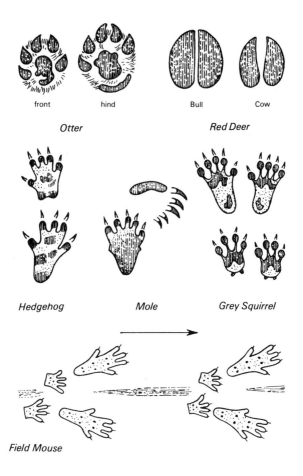

front   hind

Otter

Bull   Cow

Red Deer

Hedgehog   *Mole*   *Grey Squirrel*

Field Mouse

Poisonous Plants

Many plants are poisonous if eaten in large quantities. Some can make you very ill but not fatally. Some taste so nasty that not enough is likely to be eaten to cause any but the mildest symptoms. There are some plants which are extremely poisonous even in small amounts and these are listed below.

Garden plants
Castor oil plant (a house-plant)
Daphne laureola (spurge laurel)

Daphne mezereon (spurge olive)
Delphinium
Lily of the valley

Wild plants
Black bryony
Black nightshade
Deadly nightshade
Fool's parsley
Foxglove
Hemlock
Henbane
Monkshood (Aconite)
Spindle tree
Thornapple
White bryony
Woody nightshade
Yew

Deadly Poisonous Fungi
Death cap (Amanita phalloides). The most dangerous of all. It is quite common. The cap is pale yellowish with a slightly green tinge. Gills white. The stipe has a skirt-like ring and there is a basal bag (volva). It is found in woods, especially oak and beech.
Panther Cap (Amanita pantherina). Smoky-brown cap with white warts or patches. Common.
Destroying Angel (Amanita virosa). Wholly white. Rare.
Fool's Mushroom (Amanita verna). Rare.

Poisonous Fungi, Not Usually Deadly
Yellow Staining Mushroom. Can be mistaken for the Field Mushroom, and is not uncommon. Is detected by the bright yellow stain at the extreme base when picked. Can cause unpleasant symtoms.
Fly Agaric. Red cap with white warts or blotches. Fairly common.

*Never attempt to eat these poisonous mushrooms (from left to right):
Death Cap, Fly Agaric, Devil Boletus, False Blusher*

Some Common Trees

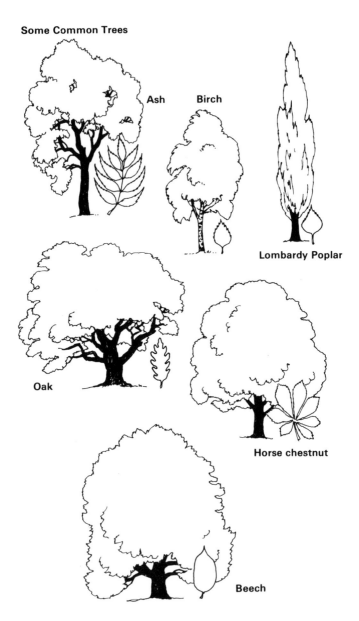

Ash

Birch

Lombardy Poplar

Oak

Horse chestnut

Beech

Sycamore

Lime

Wych Elm

Alder

Sweet chestnut

Cedar

Camping Tips

An ideal camping site should have the following:
1. Level position, in lee of the wind
2. Water not too far away
3. Firewood not too far away
4. Well-drained spot
5. Good holding position for tent pegs

Before pitching your tent, ask permission. Then be sure to clear the ground of all lumps and bumps — stones, sticks and fircones. Have the opening of your tent facing south so that the sun's rays enter during the daytime. When you go, leave no rubbish behind you.

Camping sites to avoid
1. Trees — they may shed branches in the night when the temperature drops.
2. Hollows. Water collects in them when there is a rain storm.
3. Damp meadows. When the temperature drops in the night you may find yourself wreathed in mist, a chilling experience.
4. Ants nests.

Fire-making
First get permission. Never make an open fire on a forestry site — use your stove. Do not let your fire get out of control and be utterly certain that it is extinguished when you leave. Rake over the ashes and give it a good dousing. If you have a nylon tent, remember that flying sparks can ruin it.

There are many ways of making a camp fire and of supporting the pots and pans. One method is to place two logs side by side and build the fire between them. The pots are then rested on top. You need tinder for lighting the fire — birch bark is very good for this. Softwoods (conifers) are best for kindling. They burn quickly but soon die out. Hardwoods are needed for firewood as they generally burn slowly enough for cooking. Not all hardwoods are suitable, though, as the table below will show.

Type of wood	Burning qualities
Apple	Burns well; gives off a sweet smell
Ash	Best of all
Beech	Excellent; burns green or dry
Birch	Burns quickly; use bark as tinder
Elder	Gives off acrid smoke
Holly	Fierce burner, green or dry
Lime	Good slow burner
Maple	Good slow burner
Oak	Good slow burner
Plane	Good slow burner
Sycamore	Good slow burner
Yew	Hard to start but then a good slow burner

Remember, never tear wood from a living tree. It can cause damage to the tree and will not burn.

Sport

Olympic Games

The Olympic Games were revived in 1896. They are held every four years at a place fixed by the International Olympic Committee. Cancellation does not affect the numbered sequence of the Games — thus, the Games held in Mexico City in 1968 are numbered XIX, although three meetings (Berlin in 1916, Tokyo — afterwards allotted to Helsinki — in 1940 and London in 1944) were not held because of World Wars I and II. The full list is as follows:

I	1896 Athens	XII	1940 Tokyo, Helsinki
II	1900 Paris	XIII	1944 London
III	1904 St. Louis	XIV	1948 London
IV	1908 London	XV	1952 Helsinki
V	1912 Stockholm	XVI	1956 Melbourne
VI	1916 Berlin	XVII	1960 Rome
VII	1920 Antwerp	XVIII	1964 Tokyo
VIII	1924 Paris	XIX	1968 Mexico
IX	1928 Amsterdam	XX	1972 Munich
X	1932 Los Angeles	XXI	1976 Montreal
XI	1936 Berlin	XXII	1980 Moscow

The Winter Olympics were started in 1924 and their venues are as follows:

I	1924 Chamonix	VII	1956, Cortina, Italy
II	1928 St. Moritz	VIII	1960 Squaw Valley, California
III	1932 Lake Placid		
IV	1936 Garmisch-Partenkirchen	IX	1964 Innsbruck
		X	1968 Grenoble
V	1948 St. Moritz	XI	1972 Sapporo, Japan
VI	1952 Oslo	XII	1976 Innsbruck
		XIII	1980 Lake Placid, U.S.A.

Gold Medals

The most individual gold medals won by an Olympics competitor is ten, by Raymond Clarence Ewry (U.S.A.) (1874-1937). The medals were for the Standing High, Long and Triple Jumps in 1900, 1904, 1906 and 1908.

The most gold medals won at one Games was five, by Paavo Johannes Nurmi (Finland) (1897-1973) in 1924. The most individual gold medals won at one Games was four, by Alvin C. Kraenzlein (U.S.A.) (1876-1928) in 1900 in the 60 m., 110 m. hurdles, 200 m. hurdles and long jump.

The most Olympic medals won in men's events was 12 (nine gold and three silver) by Paavo Nurmi (Finland) in 1920, 1924 and 1928.

The most individual gold medals won by a woman was seven, by the gymnast Vera Caslavska-Odlozil (Czechoslovakia): three in 1964 and four (one shared) in 1968.

The most Olympic medals won by a woman was 18, by the gymnast Larissa Latynina. She was in three winning teams and won six individual gold medals in 1956, 1960 and 1964. She also won five silver and four bronze medals making a total of 18 medals, a record for either sex in any sport.

The nation winning the greatest number of medals for all Olympic events for the Summer Games (1896-1980) and the Winter Games (1924-1980) is the U.S.A. with 660 gold, 511 silver and 1,615 bronze medals.

World Records in Athletics (Men)
(*denotes awaiting ratification)

Track events	Holder	Time Hr. Min. Sec.
RUNNING		
100 metres	J. R. Hines (U.S.A.)	9.95
200 metres	P. Mennea (Italy)	19.72
400 metres	L. E. Evans (U.S.A.)	43.86
800 metres	S. Coe (G.B.)	1:41.72*
1,000 metres	S. Coe (G.B.)	2:12.18*
1,500 metres	S. Ovett (G.B.)	3:31.36
1 mile	S. Coe (G.B.)	3:47.33
2,000 metres	J. G. Walker (New Zealand)	4:51.4
3,000 metres	H. Rono (Kenya)	7:32.1
5,000 metres	H. Rono (Kenya)	13:06.2
10,000 metres	H. Rono (Kenya)	27:22.4
20,000 metres	J. Hermens (Netherlands)	57:24.2
25,000 metres	T. Seko (Japan)	1 hr.13:55.8
30,000 metres	T. Seko (Japan)	1 hr.29:18.8*
HURDLES		
110 metres	R. Nehemiah (U.S.A.)	12.93
400 metres	E. C. Moses (U.S.A.)	47.13
3,000 metres steeplechase	H. Rono (Kenya)	8:05.37
RELAYS		
4x100 metres	U.S.A. National Team (3.9.77)	38.03
4x200 metres	Univ. of S. California Team (27.5.78)	1:20.26
4x400 metres	U.S.A. National Team (20.10.68)	2:56.16
4x800 metres	U.S.S.R. Team (13.8.78)	7:08.1
4x1,500 metres	West German Team (17.8.77)	14:38.8

Field events	Holder	Distance Metres
High Jump	G. Wessig (E. Germany)	2.36
Pole Vault	V. Poliakov (U.S.S.R.)	5.81*
Long Jump	R. Beamon (U.S.A.)	8.90
Triple Jump	J. C. de Oliveira (Brazil)	17.89
Shot Putt	U. Beyer (E. Germany)	22.15
Discus Throw	W. Schmidt (E. Germany)	71.16
Hammer Throw	Y. Sedykh (U.S.S.R.)	80.80
Javelin Throw	F. Paragi (Hungary)	96.72
Decathlon	G. Kratschmer (W. Germany)	8,649 points

World Records in Athletics (Women)

Track events	Holder	Time Hr. Min. Sec.
RUNNING		
100 metres	M. Oelsner (now Goehr) (E. Germany)	10.88
200 metres	M. Koch (E. Germany)	21.71
400 metres	M. Koch (E. Germany)	48.60
800 metres	N. Olizarenko (U.S.S.R.)	1:53.43
1,500 metres	T. Kazankina (U.S.S.R.)	3:52.47
1 mile	M. Decker (U.S.A.)	4:21.68
3,000 metres	L. Bragina (U.S.S.R.)	8:27.12
5,000 metres	P. Fudge (G.B.)	15:14.51
10,000 metres	L. Olofsson (Denmark)	31:45.35
RELAYS		
4x100 metres	East German Team (1.8.80)	41.60
4x200 metres	East German Team (9.8.80)	1:28.15
4x400 metres	East German National Team (31.7.76)	3:19.23
4x800 metres	U.S.S.R. National Team (16.8.76)	7:52.3

Field events	Holder	Distance Metres
High Jump	S. Simeoni (Italy)	2.01
Long Jump	V. Bardauskiene (U.S.S.R.)	7.09
Shot Putt	I. Slupianek (E. Germany)	22.45
Discus Throw	M. Petkova (Bulgaria)	71.80
Javelin Throw	A. Todorova (Bulgaria)	71.88
Pentathlon	N. Tkachenko (U.S.S.R.)	5,083 points (1971 scoring tables)
Heptathlon	R. Neubert (E. Germany)	6,716 points

Boxing

There are two different governing bodies that recognise boxing champions: the World Boxing Association (W.B.A.) and the World Boxing Council (W.B.C.).

World Heavyweight Champions
1892 James J. Corbett (U.S.A.)
1897 Bob Fitzsimmons (G.B.)
1899 James J. Jeffries (U.S.A.)
1905 Marvin Hart (U.S.A.)
1906 Tommy Burns (Canada)
1908 Jack Johnson (U.S.A.)
1915 Jess Willard (U.S.A.)
1919 Jack Dempsey (U.S.A.)
1926 Gene Tunney (U.S.A.)
1930 Max Schmeling (German)
1932 Jack Sharkey (U.S.A.)
1933 Primo Carnera (Italy)
1934 Max Baer (U.S.A.)
1935 James J. Braddock (U.S.A.)
1937 Joe Louis (U.S.A.)
1949 Ezzard Charles (U.S.A.)
1951 Jersey Joe Walcott (U.S.A.)
1952 Rocky Marciano (U.S.A.)
1956 Floyd Patterson (U.S.A.)
1959 Ingemar Johansson (Sweden)
1960 Floyd Patterson (U.S.A.)
1961 Floyd Patterson (U.S.A.)
1961 Sonny Liston (U.S.A.)
1964 Muhammad Ali (formerly Cassius Clay) (U.S.A.)
1965 Ernie Terrel (U.S.A.) (W.B.A.), until 1967
1968 Jimmy Ellis (U.S.A.) (W.B.A.)
1970 Joe Frazier (U.S.A.) (undisputed)
1973 George Foreman (U.S.A.)
1974 Muhammad Ali (U.S.A.)
1978 Leon Spinks (U.S.A.) (W.B.A.) Ken Norton (U.S.A.) (W.B.C.)
1978 Muhammad Ali (U.S.A.) (W.B.A.) Larry Holmes (U.S.A.) (W.B.C.)
1979 John Tate (U.S.A.) (W.B.A.)
1980 Mike Weaver (U.S.A.) (W.B.A.)

Current World Title Holders (W.B.C.)

Light Heavyweight	Matthew Saad Mohammed (formerly Matt Franklin) (U.S.A.)
Middleweight	Marvin Hagler (U.S.A.)
Light Middleweight	Wilfredo Benitez (U.S.A.)
Welterweight	Sugar Ray Leonard (U.S.A.)
Light Welterweight	Saoul Mamby (U.S.A.)
Lightweight	Alexis Arguello (Nicaragua)
Junior Lightweight	Roland Naverette (U.S.A.)
Featherweight	Salvador Sanchez (Mexico)
Light Featherweight	Wilfredo Gomez (U.S.A.)
Bantamweight	Lupe Pintor (Mexico)
Flyweight	Antonio Avelar (Mexico)
Light Flyweight	Hilario Zapata (Panama)

Current World Title Holders (W.B.A.)

Light Heavyweight	Mike Spinks (U.S.A.)
Middleweight	Marvin Hagler (U.S.A.)
Light Middleweight	title vacant
Welterweight	Sugar Ray Leonard (U.S.A.)
Light Welterweight	Aaron Pryor (U.S.A.)
Lightweight	Claude Noel (Trinidad)
Junior Lightweight	Sam Serrano (Puerto Rico)
Featherweight	Eusebio Pedroza (Panama)
Light Featherweight	Sergio Palmar (Argentina)
Bantamweight	Jeff Chandler (U.S.A.)
Flyweight	Juan Herrira (Mexico)
Light Flyweight	Hwanjin Kim (Korea)

Equestrian Events

World Show Jumping Champions (Men)
1966 Pierre d'Oriola (France), on 'Pomone'
1970 David Broome (G.B.), on 'Beethoven'
1974 Hartwig Steenken (W. Germany), on 'Simona'
1978 Gerd Wiltfang (W. Germany), on 'Roman'

Olympic Show Jumping Champions (Men)

Individual	Team
1968 William Steinkraus (U.S.A.), on 'Snowbound'	Canada
1972 Graziano Mancinelli (Italy), on 'Ambassador'	W. Germany
1976 Alwin Schockemöhle (W. Germany), on 'Warwick Rex'	France
1980 J. Kowakzyk (Poland), on 'Artemor'	

Association Football

European Cup Winners

1956 Real Madrid	1969 A.C. Milan
1957 Real Madrid	1970 Feyenoord
1958 Real Madrid	1971 Ajax Amsterdam
1959 Real Madrid	1972 Ajax Amsterdam
1960 Real Madrid	1973 Ajax Amsterdam
1961 Benfica (Portugal)	1974 Bayern Munich
1962 Benfica (Portugal)	1975 Bayern Munich
1963 Milan	1976 Bayern Munich
1964 Inter Milan	1977 Liverpool
1965 Inter Milan	1978 Liverpool
1966 Real Madrid	1979 Nottingham Forest
1967 Glasgow Celtic	1980 Liverpool
1968 Manchester United	1981 Liverpool

World Cup Winners

1930 Uruguay	1950 Uruguay
1934 Italy	1954 West Germany
1938 Italy	1958 Brazil

1962 Brazil
1966 England
1970 Brazil

1974 West Germany
1978 Argentina

Olympic Games Winners (amateurs)
1908 United Kingdom
1912 United Kingdom
1920 Belgium
1924 Uruguay
1928 Uruguay
1932 No competition
1936 Italy
1948 Sweden

1952 Hungary
1956 U.S.S.R.
1960 Yugoslavia
1964 Hungary
1968 Hungary
1972 Poland
1976 East Germany
1980 Czechoslovakia

Gymnastics

OLYMPIC GOLD MEDALS, COMBINED EXERCISES (MEN)

Year Individual	Team
1968 S. Kato (Japan)	Japan
1972 S. Kato (Japan)	Japan
1976 N. Adrianov (U.S.S.R.)	Japan
1980 A. Dityatin (U.S.S.R.)	U.S.S.R.

OLYMPIC GOLD MEDALS, COMBINED EXERCISES (WOMEN)

Year Individual	Team
1968 V. Caslavska (Czechoslovakia)	U.S.S.R.
1972 L. Tourischeva (U.S.S.R.)	U.S.S.R.
1976 N. Comaneci (Romania)	U.S.S.R
1980 E. Davidova (U.S.S.R.)	U.S.S.R.

Horse Racing

PRIX DE L'ARC DE TRIOMPHE (RUN AT LONGCHAMP, PARIS)

Year Winning Horse	Jockey
1970 Sassafras	Y. Saint-Martin
1971 Mill Reef	G. Lewis
1972 San San	F. Head
1973 Rheingold	L. Piggott
1974 Allez France	Y. Saint-Martin
1975 Star Appeal	G. Starkey
1976 Ivanjica	F. Head
1977 Alleged	L. Piggott
1978 Alleged	L. Piggott
1979 Three Troikas	F. Head
1980 Detroit	P. Eddery
1981 Gold River	L. Gary Moore

Lawn Tennis

Wimbledon Championships—Men's Singles

1946 Y. Petra	1964 R. Emerson
1947 J. A. Kramer	1965 R. Emerson
1948 R. Falkenburg	1966 M. Santana
1949 F. R. Schroeder	1967 J. Newcombe
1950 J. E. Patty	1968 (1st open). R. Laver
1951 R. Savitt	1969 R. Laver
1952 E. A. Sedgman	1970 J. Newcombe
1953 E. V. Seixas	1971 J. Newcombe
1954 J. Drobny	1972 S. R. Smith
1955 M. A. Trabert	1973 J. Kodes
1956 L. A. Hoad	1974 J. Connors
1957 L. A. Hoad	1975 A. Ashe
1958 A. J. Cooper	1976 B. Borg
1959 A. Olmedo	1977 B. Borg
1960 N. Fraser	1978 B. Borg
1961 R. Laver	1979 B. Borg
1962 R. Laver	1980 B. Borg
1963 E. McKinley	1981 J. McEnroe

Wimbledon Championships—Women's Singles

1946 Miss P. Betz	1965 Miss M. Smith
1947 Miss M. Osborne	1966 Mrs. B. J. King
1948 Miss A. Brough	1967 Mrs. B. J. King
1949 Miss A. Brough	1968 (1st open) Mrs. B. J. King
1950 Miss A. Brough	1969 Mrs. P. F. Jones
1951 Miss D. Hart	1970 Mrs. B. M. Court
1952 Miss M. Connolly	1971 Miss E. Goolagong
1953 Miss M. Connolly	1972 Mrs. B. J. King
1954 Miss M. Connolly	1973 Mrs. B. J. King
1955 Miss A. Brough	1974 Miss C. Evert
1956 Miss S. Fry	1975 Mrs. B. J. King
1957 Miss A. Gibson	1976 Miss C. Evert
1958 Miss A. Gibson	1977 Miss S. V. Wade
1959 Miss M. Bueno	1978 Miss M. Navratilova
1960 Miss M. Bueno	1979 Miss M. Navratilova
1961 Miss A. Mortimer	1980 Mrs. E. Corley (née
1962 Miss K. Susman	Goolagong)
1963 Miss M. Smith	1981 Mrs. C. Lloyd (née Evert)
1964 Miss M. Bueno	

Ice Skating

Olympic Champions

Figure Skating (Men)   1972 O. Nepela (Czechoslovakia)
1976 J. Curry (G.B.)
1980 R. Cousins (G.B.)

Figure Skating (Women)	1972 B. Schuba (Austria)
	1976 D. Hamill (U.S.A.)
	1980 A. Pötzch (E. Germany)

Pairs Skating	1972 Alexei Ulanov and Irina Rodnina (U.S.S.R.)
	1976 Alexandr Zaitsev and Irina Rodnina (U.S.S.R.)
	1980 Alexandr Zaitsev and Irina Rodnina (U.S.S.R.)

World Champions
Figure Skating (Men)   1976 J. Curry (G.B.)
1977 V. Kovalev (U.S.S.R.)
1978 C. Tickner (U.S.A.)
1979 V. Kovalev (U.S.S.R)
1980 J. Hoffmann (E. Germany)
1981 S. Hamilton (U.S.A.)

Motor Racing
World Drivers' Championship (Formula One)
1970 Jochen Rindt (Germany)
1971 Jackie Stewart (G.B.)
1972 Emerson Fittipaldi (Brazil)
1973 Jackie Stewart (G.B.)
1974 Emerson Fittipaldi (Brazil)
1975 Niki Lauda (Austria)
1976 James Hunt (G.B.)
1977 Niki Lauda (Austria)
1978 Mario Andretti (U.S.A.)
1979 Jody Scheckter (South Africa)
1980 Alan Jones (Australia)
1981 Nelson Piquét (Brazil)

Ski-Jumping
1980 Olympic Champion, 70-Metres Hill   T. Innauer (Austria)
90-Metres Hill   J. Törmänen (Finland)

Swimming—World Records (Men)

Event	Holder	Time Min. Sec.
FREESTYLE		
100 metres	A. Gaines (U.S.A.)	49.36
200 metres	A. Gaines (U.S.A.)	1:49.16
400 metres	P. Szmidt (Canada)	3:50.49
800 metres	V. Sainikov (U.S.S.R.)	7:56.49
1,500 metres	V. Sainkov (U.S.S.R.)	14:58.27
BACKSTROKE		
100 metres	J. Naber (U.S.A.)	55.49
200 metres	J. Naber (U.S.A.)	1:59.19
BREASTSTROKE		
100 metres	G. Moerken (W. Germany)	1:02.86
200 metres	D. Wilkie (G.B.)	2:15.11
BUTTERFLY		
100 metres	W. Paulus (U.S.A.)	53.81
200 metres	C. Beardsley (U.S.A.)	1:58.21
INDIVIDUAL MEDLEY		
200 metres	A. Baumann (Canada)	2:02.78
400 metres	J. Vassallo (U.S.A.)	4:20.05

Alpine Skiing

Olympic Champions 1980 (Men)
Downhill	L. Stock (Austria)
Slalom	I. Stenmark (Sweden)
Giant Slalom	I. Stenmark (Sweden)

Olympic Champions 1980 (Women)
Downhill	A. Moser (Austria)
Slalom	H. Wenzel (Liechtenstein)
Giant Slalom	H. Wenzel (Liechtenstein)

Science and Technology

Electronics

Electronics is a branch of physics or electrical engineering closely connected to the science of electricity. When electrons move, along a wire for instance, they form an electric current which can heat, light and drive motors. By the use of electronics the flow of electrons is controlled in more complex ways. Electronic devices include thermionic valves, transistors, integrated circuits, photoelectric cells, cathode ray tubes and X-ray tubes. Electronics makes possible such things as radio, television, record players and tape recorders, radar, computers, pocket calculators and digital quartz watches.

Electromagnetic Radiation

Gamma rays, X-rays, ultra-violet rays, visible light, infra-red radiation and radio waves are all forms of electromagnetic radiation. The waves all travel at the same speed of approximately 300,000,000 metres/second. Electromagnetism is fundamental in the operation of many modern inventions, including radio and television, telephones, radar, and electric motors and generators.

Radio and Television

Radio wavelengths are measured in metres, frequencies in kilocycles per second (kc/s) and Megacycles per second (Mc/s). One Megacycle = 1,000 kilocycles. Higher frequencies are necessary for good quality reproduction. Radio waves in use are shown in the table below.

Frequency	Wavelengths	Wavelength range	Frequency range
Low	Long waves	Above 600 m.	Below 500 kc/s
Medium	Medium waves	200-600 m.	500-1,500 kc/s
			3,750 kc/s-30 Mc/s
High	Short waves	10-80 m.	
Very high	Ultra-short	Band I 4.41-7.32 m.	41-68 Mc/s
(V.H.F.)	waves	Band II 3-3.43 m.	87.5-100 Mc/s
		Band III 1.39-1.72 m.	174-216 Mc/s
Ultra-high		Band IV 51-63 cm.	475-585 Mc/s
(U.H.F.)		Band V 31-49 cm.	610-960 Mc/s
	Micro-waves	7.5 mm.-15 cm.	2,000-40,000 Mc/s

Radio

How is a radio broadcast made? A microphone must first pick up the sound waves—a singer's voice for example—and change them into electric current. The current consists of audio-signals which represent the varying sounds made by the singer. It flows along a wire to an amplifier which magnifies these oscillations and then on to a transmitter which amplifies them still further. The transmitting aerial sends out through space a strong, steady wave called a carrier wave. This is modulated by the impression of the audio-signals representing the singer's voice. The receiving aerial of the radio set picks up some of the transmitted waves which set up a minute current in it. The current is conducted to the radio receiver where it is amplified by transistors. The audio-signals are then converted by the loudspeaker into sound waves.

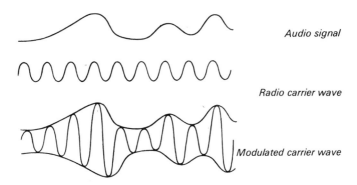

Audio signal

Radio carrier wave

Modulated carrier wave

Television

Television is the transmission of visible images by means of radio waves. The scene in front of a television camera is converted into electrical impulses by the camera tube. This has a face plate coated on the inside with a light-sensitive substance in the form of masses of minute dots. At the other end of the tube an electron gun shoots out a beam of electrons which strike the photosensitive area. Electric current in coils of wire cause the beam to flick backwards and forwards at tremendous speed, moving from the top of the screen to the bottom. As it does this the tiny light-sensitive dots release electrons which flow as current representing the varying tones that make up the picture. These video-signals are amplified and transmitted by radio waves in the same way as sound signals. For colour pictures three cameras are needed.

Both sound and vision are received on the same aerial. The cathode ray tube in the television set changes the signal current into a picture, acting like a television camera in reverse. The screen at the far end of the tube is coated with a fluorescent material which glows when bombarded with electrons. An electron beam moves across the screen in the same way and at the same speed as the beam in the camera, giving rise to a reproduction of the original scene.

Computers

A computer is an electronic machine which can handle information and solve problems at lightning speed. Problems dealing with words are solved by converting them to numbers. A computer differs from a simple calculating machine in having a large *memory,* i.e. it can store information (*data*) and use it later. There are special machines for putting data into the computer (*input*). They may work with punched cards, magnetic tape or discs. When the calculations have been performed on the data the results emerge from an output machine, such as a line-printer. Some line-printers can print over 2,000 lines a minute. The input and output units are separate from the central processing unit (CPU) where the actual calculations are made. They are called *peripherals.*

The *memory* or core-store consists of thousands of tiny metal rings called *ferrite cores.* Each of these can be magnetised. When the flow of magnetism in any core is in one direction it represents a value of 0. When the flow is reversed the value is 1. The individual cores are referred to as bits. A bit is short for Binary digIT. The bits are arranged in groups called *words*. The largest computers have 200,000 or more words. The size is referred to as so many *K* (short for kilo, meaning 1,000). Thus, a 4,000-word computer is said to have a 4K core-store. The method of using 1s and 0s to represent any number is called the *Binary System.* The memory remembers a number by magnetising a group of cores.

The bit-patterns may represent characters, the 0s and 1s being used like the dots and dashes of Morse Code. Bit-patterns also hold the instructions given to the computer. For example, 001 might be the code for Add, 010 might mean Subtract. There will similarly be instructions for Multiply and Divide and various others. Obviously the computer needs to identify the various words, so every word in the core-store has an *address*. The words of a 16K computer would be numbered 0-15999, since the numbering always starts with a 0 and not with a 1.

Program

A program is a series of instructions which tells the computer what it must do to the contents of specified words in the core-store in order to produce results from the data. It will also contain instructions telling the peripheral units when they must read a card or print a line. The instructions of the program are carried out in an ordered sequence and follow the steps of a 'process'.

Suppose we had three numbers (say, 150, 263 and 166) and we wanted to know their average. The process of finding an average is to add the numbers together and divide their sum by the number of numbers. In this case, adding 150, 263 and 166 together equals 579. Divide 579 by 3 and the result, 193, is the average. But you don't need a computer to do that. If, however, you had a thousand groups, each of three numbers, and had to find the average in each group, it would be a very long task to work the answers out yourself. It could be done on a computer this way:

First, each group of three numbers is punched in a separate card. This is done on a machine rather like a typewriter but which punches holes in cards instead of typing characters on paper. With room for 80 characters

114

on each card, all three numbers could be placed on the same card, say on the Left, Middle and Right. We will call the numbers on each of the 1,000 cards L, M and R. The computer has to read a card containing the data: add L, M and R; divide the sum by 3; print the result; read the next card and repeat the process until all the cards have been processed. The computer would have to be given instructions something like this:

1.	Set the bits in Word 200 equal to 3	$W200 = 3$
2.	Read the next card	
3.	Convert the numbers L, M and R on the card to their binary form and copy them into Words 201, 202 and 203 respectively	$W201 = L$ $W202 = M$ $W203 = R$
4.	Add the contents of Word 201 to the contents of Word 203	$W203 =$ $R + M$
5.	Add the contents of Word 202 to the contents of Word 203	$W203 =$ $(R + M) + L$
6.	Divide the contents of Word 203 by the contents of Word 200	$W203 =$ $(R + M + L) \div 3$
7.	Print the contents of Word 203 in decimal form	
8.	Has the last card been read? If NO, go back to instruction 2 If YES, go on to instruction 9	
9.	Stop	

In instruction 3, by 'copying' the numbers L, M and R into Words 201, 202 and 203 each time a card is read, the new numbers replace the old ones whose average has been calculated. Do you see, too, that instruction 1 is only obeyed once, even before the first card has been read? In this way, Word 200 stays at 3 whilst every one of the cards is read so it can be used each time to do the division sum. Instructions 2 to 8 are obeyed each time a card is read so that in carrying out the program the computer performs 7 instructions, 1,000 times plus instruction 1 once at the beginning and instruction 9 once at the end. That is, 7,002 instructions in all.

This program must itself be put into the computer before the data cards are read. To do this, the instructions are written in a programming language, punched into cards and then fed into the core-store via the card-reader. Each instruction is stored in a separate word.

A program, therefore, works by the contents of some words, acting as instructions, operating on the contents of other words, representing data. Any program can be written to do any particular job. It is important to understand that a computer does not 'think' in the way a human being thinks. It will do only what it is instructed to do, no more and no less. Programs must therefore be written very carefully and accurately. If the computer is given a wrong instruction, it will carry it out obediently but the results will be wrong.

Programming Languages
The way in which instructions have to be written vary from one computer to another. There are three types of languages:

(i) Machine orders

(ii) Basic autocodes

(iii) High level autocodes

In machine orders, the programmer (who writes the program) has to write the instructions in their coded number form and has to work out all the addresses himself. This method is very rarely used.

In basic autocodes, programming is made easier by using mnemonics such as A for Add and MPY for Multiply instead of the number codes, and using symbolic names for data areas instead of working out the addresses of words. These languages need a special program of their own, called a 'compiler', to translate the autocode into machine orders. The compiler also works out which words are to be used to hold the instructions and which to hold the data.

High level autocodes can be used for writing programs which will run on any computer so long as the appropriate compiler is available to translate the code into the particular computer's machine-orders. 'Statements' are written, usually in the form of equations like $AVERAGE = (L + M + R) \div 3$. In addition to working out words for holding instructions and data, the compiler-programs even work out what instructions are necessary to obey the statements because the computer itself still has to have detailed instructions like those in the example program given earlier. There are several high-level languages in common use: FORTRAN, ALGOL, COBOL, PL/1 and BASIC. Each has features that makes it most suitable for a particular task. FORTRAN, for example, was designed for scientific work and COBOL for commercial data-processing.

SOME IMPORTANT DEVELOPMENTS IN SCIENCE AND TECHNOLOGY

Integrated Circuits

Electronic circuits can be extremely complex. If the component parts are connected with wire considerable time will have been taken to join them all together, and the end result may look like quite a tangle. In the 1950s the problem of wiring up complicated circuits was remedied with the introduction of printed circuits. The components were fastened to a base of insulating material and the 'wiring' was chemically printed on it. The basic principles of the printed circuit were used in the development of integrated circuits.

Silicon Chips

An integrated circuit consists of a chip of pure silicon buried in a plastic bar. Etched into the silicon are small amounts of chemical impurities. The areas of impurity act as the electronic components, such as transistors, in conventional circuits. The whole thing is only a few millimetres square. Equipment that contains integrated circuits is therefore smaller. It costs less and uses less power than transistorised equipment. In the 1960s integrated circuits caused a revolution in electronics, just as transistors had done in the 1950s.

The silicon chip is now used in all kinds of electronic equipment including radios, TV sets and computers.

Microprocessors

In the 1970s the 'microprocessor' was developed. This consists of a single integrated circuit that can perform the mathematical tasks of a large computer but of course costs less. Microprocessors are used in pocket calculators, digital quartz watches and in operating and controlling various industrial machines.

Lasers

A laser is a device designed to give out a very narrow beam of light of very pure colour. The word laser stands for Light Amplification by Stimulated Emission of Radiation. Scientists developed the laser during the 1950s and early 1960s.

From an ordinary light source such as a light bulb or the sun, light streams out uniformly in all directions. Thus the further we are from the source the fainter the light appears. Laser beams on the other hand spread only slightly as they travel. For example, a beam may be only 1 mm. in diameter at the point where it leaves the laser and at a distance of 10 metres it may spread to only 0.5 cm. in diameter.

Extremely high intensity laser beams can be produced as continuous sources or pulsed in powerful flashes. The most powerful pulsed laser flashes will vapourise any known material—they can even bore holes in a diamond, the hardest substance known.

Early Lasers

The first successful laser used an artificially grown crystal of ruby. Ruby consists of aluminium oxide in which a few of the aluminium ions have been replaced by *ions* of chromium which give rubies their characteristic red colour. (An ion is an electrically charged atom.) When the chromium ions become excited (energised) by a brilliant flash of light they emit their excess of energy in the form of light. When the ruby is placed between two partially transparent parallel mirrors some of this emitted light is reflected off a mirror and passes back through the crystal to be reflected by the opposite mirror. And thus it goes, back and forth, on an on. When this radiation interacts with another excited chromium ion the radiation is amplified.

This mirror system leads to a continuous build-up of intensity with very large numbers of excited ions contributing their excess energy to the beam which emerges from the mirror at the end of the ruby as a pencil-like flash of red light. As some of the energy given out by the chromium ions appears as heat in the ruby crystal prolonged operation is not possible, the duration of the illuminating flash being only about a thousandth of a second. The power of the first operating laser, based on this principle, was 10,000 watts. Since then the ruby laser has been developed to generate ten thousand million watts.

Gas

Another kind of laser that has been developed is the gas laser. An electric current is passed through a tube of gas which has mirrors at each end. Most gas lasers produce a continuous beam of light.

Liquids

Liquid lasers consist of a glass tube containing a dye dissolved in methanol or a similar liquid. Flash tubes cause the atoms of the dye to emit laser light. Different dyes produce different frequencies. A liquid laser can produce both bursts of light and continuous light.

Semi-conductor lasers consist of a block having two layers of semi-conductor, each having a different electric charge. When electric current is passed through the block laser light streams out from the joint between the two semi-conductors.

How lasers are used

Lasers have many uses for scientists and technologists. A laser beam can be used to bore a hole through a sheet of hard metal in less than a second. Because it can be focused by a lens to an extremely narrow beam it can shape and weld tiny metal parts very accurately. Surgeons have used laser beams very successfully in repairing detached retinas in eye operations.

In the field of communications the laser offers an enormous potential. Laser beams can transmit sound and television signals in a similar way to radio waves. The laser beam has a great advantage. Its high frequency (10^{15} cycles/second) enables it to carry much more information than a radio wave can.

Holography

Like photography, holography makes a picture of a scene or object. A photograph shows an object as seen from the position of the camera. It cannot give a three-dimensional view of the object—but a hologram can. Holograms only became possible when the laser was invented. A characteristic of laser light is that it is coherent, i.e. the light waves are in phase with one another and all of the same wavelength. When coherent light strikes an object the waves from the more distant parts of it will lag behind waves from closer areas, and it is this information about lagging and leading waves that are recorded on a hologram.

Light from a laser is split into two beams. One is reflected from the object to be recorded. The other, a reference beam, is reflected from a mirror. The two reflected beams strike the recording plate where they interact together, or *interfere.* Since a camera has not been used this does not produce a photograph. But when coherent light is shone on the plate and we look through it, the original image appears—in three dimensions. The picture changes when we move our head just as if we were looking at the original scene. By using three laser beams giving different frequencies corresponding to the three primary colours (red, green and blue), it is possible to reconstruct a scene in full colour.

Bionics

Bionics is popularly supposed to be concerned with the development of artificial body parts that have superhuman powers. But that idea arose purely out of science fiction. Bionics is in reality the study of the special abilities of various living organisms, the knowledge gained being applied in solving engineering problems. For example, a new kind of ship's propeller was designed in 1964 by a French engineer based on a fish's tail. The advantages over an ordinary propeller are its high thrust at low speed, being able to function in shallow water and not getting fouled up with seaweed.

Genetic Engineering

Inherited characteristics in living organisms are transmitted by the genes. Genes are differentiated segments found along the length of a chromosome. Chromosomes are long, threadlike molecules found in every cell nucleus. A single chromosome may carry thousands of genes, each with its own specific structure. Genes are composed of a substance called DNA which carries the hereditary information.

In sexual reproduction exchanges and reassortment of the chromosomes take place between individuals of the same species. Scientists have now learned to break down the species barriers. Techniques have been devised for transferring genes from one organism to another. This is known as genetic engineering. The process involves splicing (joining) DNA from two organisms to form one piece of DNA.

Parapsychology

Parapsychology is a branch of psychology that deals with extrasensory perception (ESP). ESP denotes the awareness of something without using the known sense organs. It may manifest in different forms. *Telepathy* is the extrasensory perception of another person's thoughts. *Clairvoyance* is the extrasensory perception of an object or event. *Precognition* is the awareness of a future event. Another apparent phenomenon studied by parapsychologists is *psychokinesis* (PK), the movement of physical objects by the power of the mind.

The term ESP was coined by Dr. J. B. Rhine who set up the first parapsychology laboratory, in 1935, at Duke University in the U.S.A. To test for the existence of ESP Rhine developed card-guessing techniques and applied the mathematics of probability to the results. There were 25 cards in the pack, each card bearing one of five geometrical shapes: star, circle, square, cross and wavy lines. Subjects had to guess the order of the cards when they were concealed from view. The Duke University team devised ways of controlling experiments to eliminate the possibility of subjects picking up clues about the card order. Nevertheless certain subjects consistently scored higher than five out of 25 (the score one would expect if chance were the only factor operating). When a particular subject scores highly in a very large number of trials the odds of this happening by chance alone are very great indeed. Experimenters elsewhere were able to obtain similar results with a few people of apparent psychic ability.

Now if ESP exists, as the experiments suggest, it goes against the mechanical laws of science and naturally Rhine's work met with considerable opposition. Some critics dismissed the results of all the major ESP experiments on the grounds that they could have been produced by error or fraud on the part of the subjects or the experimenters. Modern technology, however, has been instrumental in eliminating human error and fraud in the experiments.

Transport Facts and Figures

Land

The first two successful motorcars were built in 1885 by Karl-Friedrich Benz at Manheim, Germany. They had three wheels and were driven by a single cylinder petrol engine. The maximum speed attained was about 16 km/hr. One of these cars is on show at the German Museum, Munich.

The fastest-ever wheel-driven vehicle was driven by Sir Donald Campbell, a British engineer, in 1964. The highest speed reached was 691 km/hr. His car, 'The Bluebird', measured 9.1 m. in length and weighed 4,354 kg. It was powered by a Bristol-Siddeley Proteus 705 gas turbine engine.

The Bluebird

The fastest-ever jet-engined car attained 988 km/hr. Called 'The Spirit of America-Sonic I', it was driven by Norman Craig Breedlove on Bonneville Salt Flats, Utah, U.S.A., in 1965.

The highest speed ever attained by a vehicle on land was 1,190 km/hr by a rocket-engined three-wheeled car, 'The Budweiser Rocket'. It was driven by Stan Barrett at Edwards Air Force Base, California in 1979. The official land speed record is 1,001.5 km/hr, set by Gary Gabelich in 1970 in 'The Blue Flame' which was rocket-powered.

The world's longest limousine is the American Oldsmobile Tornado of 1968. It has six wheels, nine doors and is 8.53 m. long.

The car longest in production is the Volkswagen 'Beetle' series. First produced in 1938, production stopped in West Germany in 1978.

The earliest bicycle was built in 1839-40 by Kirkpatrick Macmillan of Dumfries, Scotland. It is now in the Science Museum, London.

The earliest motorised bicycle was built in 1885 by Gottlieb Daimler. Its maximum speed was 19 km/hr.

The first road steam locomotive was patented in 1802 by Richard Trevithick. His first steam locomotive ran at the Coalbrookdale Iron Works in Shropshire in 1803 and was the first to run on rails. The first passenger-carrying railway was the Oystermouth Railway which ran from 1906 between Swansea and Oystermouth (in Wales). Horses were used to pull the wagons.

The first public railway to use steam locomotives was the Stockton and Darlington line which opened in 1825. The 'Locomotion', designed by George Stephenson, could pull 49 tonnes at a speed of 24 km/hr. At first only goods wagons were used on the line. The first electric railway was Werner von Siemen's 548 m long track at the Berlin Trades Exhibition in 1879.

The rail speed record, attained in 1974, is held by the U.S. Federal Railroad Administration's L.I.M.R.V. (Linear Induction Motor Research Vehicle). Running on the 10 km Pueblo test track in Colorado it reached 410 km/h. The world's largest railway station is the Grand Central Terminal at New York which covers 19 hectares on two levels with 41 tracks on the upper level and 26 on the lower.

The most extensive underground railway in the world is that of London Transport, 130.3 km of it being bored tunnel. The first section, opened in 1863, was the earliest underground railway in the world.

Water
The first successful power-driven vessel was the 'Charlotte Dundas', built in 1802 in Scotland by William Symington. The first commercially successful steam vessel service was launched by Robert Fulton with his 'Clermont' on the Hudson river in 1807.

The giant 'Great Britain' was the first propeller-driven ship to cross the Atlantic. Launched in 1843 and the largest ship of her time, she weighed 3,322.5 tonnes and was 98 m in length. The earliest turbine ship was the 'Turbinia', designed by Sir Charles Parsons and completed by 1894. She was 30.5 m long and reached a speed of 34.5 knots (64 km/hr).

The first iron-built, armour-clad battleship was H.M.S. 'Warrior', completed in 1866. The French 'La Gloire' which preceded this was built of wood though heavily armoured.

The first modern battleship was H.M.S. 'Devastation'. Guns were mounted on pivoted turrets.

The largest-ever passenger liner was Britain's 'Queen Elizabeth'. She weighed 85,016 tonnes and had a length of 314 m. Her last passenger voyage was in 1968.

The largest ship of any kind is the tanker 'Pierre Guillaumat', completed in 1977. Her length is 414.23 m, her beam is 63.05 m and she has a draught of 28.6 m.

The Pierre Guillaumat

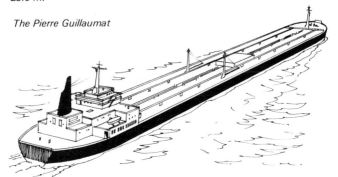

The first hovercraft passenger service was run across the Dee Estuary with Vickers-Armstrong's VA-3 in 1962. The hovercraft's speed was 60 knots (111 km/hr).

Air
The first successful balloon experiment was carried out by the Montgolfier brothers in 1783, near Lyons, France. The first manned ascents were made that same year by Pilâtre de Rozier at Paris using Montgolfier balloons.

The official altitude record for a manned balloon ascent is 34,668 m by Malcolm D. Ross and Victor E. Pratten in 1961.

The record distance covered by a manned balloon is 5001.22 km (in 137 hr 5 min 50 sec). This was achieved with the American 'Double Eagle II' which travelled from Maine, U.S.A. to Miserey in France.

The first true aeroplane was Orville and Wilbur Wright's 'Flyer I'. The first flight was in 1903 at Kitty Hawk, N.C., U.S.A., when Orville Wright flew a distance of 36.5 m at 48 km/hr at an altitude of 2.5–3.5 m for about 12 seconds. The aircraft was driven by a 4-cylinder petrol motor of 12 hp.

The first man to fly across the English Channel was the Frenchman Louis Blériot in his 'Blériot XI' monoplane.

The first non-stop crossing of the North Atlantic by air was achieved by Capt.John Alcock and Lt. Arthur Whitten Brown in a Vickers Vimy bomber in 1919.

The first aircraft turbojet engine was that of the British designer Sir Frank Whittle which was tested in 1937 and later powered the Gloucester Meteor aircraft. The first flight by an aeroplane powered by a turbojet engine was in 1939. The aeroplane was designed by the German pioneer designer Professor Ernst Heinkel and was called the Heinkel HE 178.

The first supersonic flight was in 1947 when Capt. Charles Yeager flew over the Edwards Air Force Base in California, U.S.A. in a Bell XS-1 rocket-powered aeroplane at 1,078 km/hr and at an altitude of 12,800 m.

The fastest airliner in the world is the Concorde SST, introduced into commercial airline service simultaneously by Air France and British Airways in 1969. The record time for the New York–London service was 2 hr 59 min 14 sec, averaging 1,876.54 km/hr, set in 1980.

The aircraft holding the official air speed record (3,530 km/hr) is the U.S.A.F. Lockheed SR-71A 'Blackbird' reconnaissance aircraft, first flown in 1964. It also holds the sustained altitude record of 26,213 m.

The fastest-known aeroplane in history is the North American X-15 rocket-powered research aircraft which was flown at a speed of 7,279 km/hr by W. J. Knight in 1967.

The X-15 Aircraft

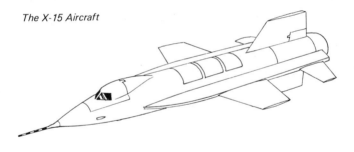

The fastest fighter in service is the Russian Mikoyan MiG-25 with a speed of 3,200 km/hr and radar and long range missiles for destroying aircraft at a distance.

The airliner with the largest capacity is the Boeing 747 'Jumbo Jet', which entered service in 1970. It can seat up to 500 passengers and has a maximum speed of 978 km/hr.

The longest non-stop scheduled passenger flight is the Pan-Am Sydney–San Francisco flight, taking 13 hr 25 min.

The largest airport in the world is the Dallas/Fort Worth Airport, Texas, U.S.A., opened in 1974. It covers 7,080 hectares and its four runways and two terminal buildings are to be increased to nine runways and 13 terminals.

The first man-powered aircraft to cross the English Channel was that of Dr. Paul MacReady in 1979. It was pedalled and piloted by Bryan Allen.

America's Space Shuttle

Spaceflight
The first man in space was Major Yuri A. Gagarin of the U.S.S.R. He reached an altitude of 327 km above the Earth and made one orbit. The first man to step on the moon's surface was Neil Armstrong, U.S. astronaut, on 21st July, 1969, following a landing in the Sea of Tranquillity.

Russia's two-man Soyuz 24 docked with the Salyut 5 spacelab during a flight lasting over 424 hours, from 7th to 25th February, 1977.

America's space shuttle, the first reusable space transporter, successfully completed its first expedition in 1981.

World Religions

Belief in supernatural powers and religious activities connected with them date from the very earliest times. Today, religion still plays a very important part in the lives of millions. Here is a brief description of the world's major religions.

Buddhism

Buddhism arose in northern India during the latter part of the 5th century B.C. Its founder was a prince named Siddhartha Gautama who became known as Gautama Buddha ('Enlightened One'). He turned away from his royal life of luxury and followed the path of religion. He lived like a beggar whilst seeking to find the cause of human suffering. After six years of fruitless search he sat down under a tree known as the Bodhi tree and at last achieved enlightenment. He discovered the 'four noble truths': that existence is sorrow; sorrow is caused by selfish desire; desire can be destroyed; it can be destroyed by following the 'noble eightfold path'. The steps on that path are: right views; right intention; right speech; right action; right livelihood; right effort; right mindfulness; and right concentration. The release so obtained would enable a person to reach *nirvana*, a state in which he loses his individuality by merging with the universal life. Until nirvana is attained, Buddhists believe that people must reincarnate again and again.

By the time of Gautama's death in 483 B.C. Buddhism was firmly established in India. From there it spread to central Asia. By 100 A.D. it had reached China, and by 500 A.D. it had spread to Japan and Korea also. Early in its history Buddhism divided into two principal forms — Theravada and Mahayana. Zen Buddhism is a form that emphasises meditation.

A statue of Buddha

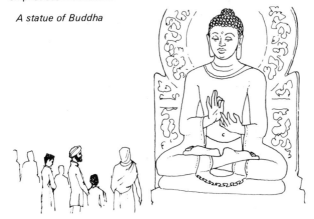

Christianity

Christianity was founded by Jesus Christ in Palestine in the first third of the 1st century. After Jesus' crucifixion, a number of his followers spread his teachings. Early in the third century the Roman Emperor Constantine became a Christian and by the end of that century Christianity was widely practised throughout the Roman Empire. Christianity is grounded on the Bible, in particular the four Gospels of the New Testament. Christians believe in one all-good, all-wise, all-powerful God who sent Jesus to the world as a Saviour. Almost all uphold the doctrine of the Trinity, i.e. the union of God the Father, Son (Jesus Christ) and Holy Ghost in one Godhead.

In 1054 A.D. a split that had been developing between Christians in western Europe and those in eastern Europe became a permanent division. The church in the west became known as the Roman Catholic Church, and the churches of Greece, Russia and other parts of eastern Europe became known as the Eastern Orthodox churches.

Another great break in the unity of Christianity came in the 16th century with the Reformation. Two major groups of reformed churches arose who refused to acknowledge the authority of the Pope—those who followed Luther and those who adopted Calvin's teachings. This Protestant movement later gave rise to a large number of Christian sects. Early in the present century a movement began which sought to unify Christians. The Ecumenical Movement, as it is known, was confined to Protestants at first but in this latter part of the 20th century the Roman Catholic Church began to take a more active part in it.

Hinduism

Hinduism began about 1500 B.C. when the Dravidian people of India were conquered by a central Asian people, the Aryans; Hinduism developed from a blend of the two cultures. The oldest Hindu scriptures are the Vedas, composed over a period of about 1,000 years from 1000 B.C. onwards.

Hindus believe in Brahma, an impersonal, all-embracing spirit working through a triad of gods—Brahma the creator, Vishnu the preserver and Siva the destroyer and generator of new life. Vishnu is considered to have been incarnated a number of times, once as Krishna, a popular deity. Numerous minor deities are worshipped, but these are all regarded as manifestations of Brahma by more educated Hindus. A basic belief is that of reincarnation of the soul, and of 'Karma', whereby a person's life is affected by his conduct in previous lives. Hindus worship within the framework of the caste system. Temple worship is almost universally performed and there are many festivals.

Islam

Islam means 'submission to the will of God', and is a religion founded by the Arabian prophet Mohammed (570–632 A.D.). The most fundamental belief of its adherents, called Moslems, is that 'There is no God but Allah, and Mohammed is his prophet'. Moslems believe in a heaven and a hell and in certain sacred scriptures said to be revealed by Allah to a line of